Bedford
Garden Club
Originals

BEDFORD
GARDEN CLUB
ORIGINALS

New York's
Eloise Luquer and Delia Marble

JUDY CULBRETH

THE
History
PRESS

Published by The History Press
Charleston, SC
www.historypress.com

Front cover: Wildflower images by Eloise Payne Luquer. *Bedford Garden Club*. Fuzzy white balls of *Cephalanthus occidentalis* (button bush), striking orange *Asclepias tuberosa* (butterfly weed), and purple *Asclepias incarnata* (swamp milkweed). *Photographs: The Frick Collection/Frick Art Reference Library Archives.*
Back cover, top: A World War I farmerette recruiting poster and James Montgomery Flagg poster for Stage Women's Group. *Library of Congress.*
Bottom: The garden of Dorothy Claire Conron Butler. *Library of Congress.*

First published 2023

Manufactured in the United States

ISBN 9781467155380

Library of Congress Control Number: 2023940692

To the Camerons of Airlie Farm.

CONTENTS

PREFACE AND ACKNOWLEDGEMENTS

Four years ago, I asked Dort Cameron, the father-in-law of my daughter Brett, how Airlie Farm got its name. I didn't realize at the time that this simple question and a look in the Camerons' attic would lead me on a rummage through history, community building, landmark gardens and an array of exceptional women from the Progressive Era.

In the first iteration of this book, the focus was on Dort's clue to follow the lives of the Three Graces of Bedford, New York—Eloise Luquer, Delia Marble and Carolena Wood. The trio, he said, "founded everything in Bedford, and Delia owned the farm."

After a time, it became apparent that the Garden Club of Bedford, New York, and The Garden Club of America were the cornerstones of two of the women's stories. These groups were the vehicles through which Eloise and Delia shaped their interests and came to the realization that they had power when they organized. The garden clubs' influence was not applicable to Quaker missionary Carolena, and I've separated her remarkable tale in a different manuscript.

Researcher Diane Bamford and Evelyne Ryan, the executive director of New York's Bedford Historical Society, offered important information and insight on the Three Graces and Bedford's history. I appreciate their valuable assistance.

Varner Redmon of the Bedford Garden Club and Kathy Crosby, the head librarian of the Brooklyn Botanic Garden, came to my aid when the book took a different turn. Varner pointed me to the Historic

Gardens of Bedford, part of The Garden Club of America collection at the Smithsonian Institution. Kathy, a longtime fan of Eloise and Delia, supplied information on Brooklyn Botanic Garden's history and some of the exquisite images of Luquer's paintings you'll find in these pages. Julie Ludwig of the Frick Collection/Frick Art Reference Library Archives provided important original letters and photographs. Kelly Crawford, the museum specialist/collections specialist at the Smithsonian's Archives of American Gardens, was ever patient when securing scans. Andrea Meyer, a department head of the Long Island Collection at the East Hampton Library, provided access to images of the Montauk Seven Sisters. I'm so grateful for the way these women shared their enthusiasm, expertise and treasures. Walter Kirkland, Cooper Smithers and Calagaz Photo and Digital Imaging aided in technical support. Banks Smither of The History Press was a champion of the book from the first query letter and through editing and publication. Ashley Hill was a thoughtful copy editor. My unofficial publicists who kindly arranged speaking engagements and promotions included Beverly Smith, Eugenia Foster, Carol Gordon, Teresa Smith, Foncie Bullard, Alison Knight, Anne Meyercord, Dana Maloney, Cele Cameron, Roy and Nancy Hoffman, Chapel Farm Collection, Jan Harayda, Sarah Finlayson, Mary Anne Mulvey and Jan Pike.

Like a nature trail, this narrative is not perfectly straight and orderly. I did substantial clearing to keep the main characters distinct. But I confess to meandering when I discovered particularly scenic beauty or interesting individuals with connections to Eloise and Delia. I hope you'll enjoy these wanderings off the path. I know, too, that when I visit public gardens, such as the famous Bellingrath Gardens in my hometown, I may make a beeline to the cascading chrysanthemums exhibit. But how can I not also stop to admire the orchids? The stories also include the women's volunteer work aside from their work with the garden club to round out the full picture of their multifaceted characters.

By the way, I don't want to be a spoiler, so the answer to my original question does not come until part II, chapter 10.

INTRODUCTION

As young women, Eloise Luquer and Delia Marble exemplified vitality and purpose. "They had vision, imagination, a strong sense of public responsibility and a love for their town," wrote the Bedford Garden Club (BGC) of New York.

The close friends lived less than one and a half miles apart in six-square-mile Bedford for almost seventy years. At the time they were born, Bedford's population was 3,697; by their deaths, it had more than doubled. But the footprint of the village hadn't changed from its six square miles. Eloise and Delia enlarged and reshaped their small community in civic, cultural and environmental ways, helping initiate and lead the District Nursing Association (the first in a rural American area), starting the local library, founding the Bedford Garden Club and establishing a nature trail (both among the first in America). Their creativity and influence didn't stop at the village green. As they matured, their reach extended to the larger world.

Eloise (1862–1947) and Delia (1868–1951) straddled the eras of late Victorianism and early Progressivism, which meant that restrictive gender roles hobbled their earliest years, while remarkable change was astir and new freedoms were available in middle age. As a way to put the breadth of the transitions in focus, note that the elder and most long-lived, Eloise, was born during the Civil War and died as rock 'n' roll was making its debut.

The women met the twentieth century as they were about to be officially termed *spinsters*, or women unlikely to marry or procreate. The social conventions of the previous century confined thirty-something never-wed women, also called old maids, to quiet, helpful work within the family, and the duo knew these expectations firsthand. A relative who lived with Eloise throughout her childhood, Sophie Berg—said to be handy with needlework— was passed around Eloise's mother's family like a favorite antique. Delia lived for forty-five years with her spinster schoolmarm aunt Susan.

If these examples were not enough to define their prospects, the law and their own loving families showed them limits in other ways. Eloise was fifty-five years old when women won the right to vote in New York State. Eloise and Delia were homeschooled for the most part, and while they turned out uncommonly literate, eloquent, organized and creative, their brothers were also given the advantage of boarding school and college. Delia's brother graduated from the U.S. Naval Academy; the two Luquer sons were awarded graduate degrees from Ivy League Columbia University.

Without the political power their male neighbors and kinfolk took for granted, the two empowered themselves. Without a voice in government, they made themselves heard. Without the richer curriculums, spheres of activity and resources that were matter-of-factly bestowed on their well-educated brothers, these bright, energetic women accomplished more than what was dreamed for them. They returned more than they were given.

It was their mutual interest in the natural world that bound their friendship and unlocked their gifts. Original founders of the Bedford Garden Club in 1911 and charter members of The Garden Club of America (GCA) in 1912, the sheltered middle-aged women began to experience new points of view, challenges and gratification while in leadership roles of these nascent garden club organizations. Meeting like-minded peers from many different places stimulated the thinking of these small-town ladies and nourished their autonomy and greatness of spirit. As an exhibition at the Smithsonian Institution pointed out, "Before the right to vote came to all women, social groups like garden clubs were one of the few ways women could band together and influence the political world."

Eloise Luquer's paintings and contributions to the science and understanding of botany earned her the sobriquet "the Audubon of Wildflowers." Her lesser-known accomplishments were shepherding America's first nature trails and, as a committee chair of GCA, helping spearhead the fundraising that established a redwood preserve in California. The GCA's Eloise Luquer Medal for special achievement in the field of botany that may include medical research, the fine arts or education is still awarded in her honor.

Delia Marble gathered some of the first specimens for New York Botanical Garden. During World War I, she and a devoted companion helped organize and implement the national prototype for a woman's land army training camp. This made Bedford the cradle of the farmerettes. The first chair of GCA's Wild Flower Preservation Committee and a president of Bedford Garden Club, Delia was recognized by the GCA for her outstanding work in conservation, bestowing on her the Francis K. Hutchinson Medal.

The Wildflower Garden at Ward-Pound Ridge Reservation in Westchester County, New York, which is maintained and undergoing restoration by local garden clubs, is named for these two friends. The BGC called them our "guiding stars." The ever-evolving patience, resourcefulness and perseverance of these "fine-minded," good-spirited women are worth recalling and emulating. Their fulfillment in being good daughters, charitable neighbors and likeable companions spilled from their families to the community and to the nation. The Bedford Graces, as they were nicknamed, truly graced their place and time.

PART I

ELOISE PAYNE LUQUER

The Audubon of Wildflowers

October 16, 1862–December 28, 1947

Born in Brooklyn but raised in the protective warmth of a country parsonage, Eloise developed a character defined by home and duty. The beloved "daughter of St. Matthew's parish" fulfilled her obligations to family, church and community with a joyful heart and fixed attention to daily responsibilities. Indeed, she outdid ordinary standards, helping create a district nursing association, a town library, one of America's first garden clubs and a nature trail in her hometown of Bedford, New York.

Eloise Payne Luquer in the 1880s, the period when she initiated her wildflower watercolors. The photograph appeared in Eloise's recollections, *Old Bedford Days. The Frick Collection/Frick Art Reference Library Archives.*

She was not, however, merely what family, local Episcopalians and neighbors expected. All her childhood, she observed firsthand the limitations of benign domesticity in the person of Sophie Berg, a ward of her family for at least twenty-five years. After age three, Eloise never lived more than a mile from the rectory. Although home was her sanctuary, the fate of the dependent homebody, such as Sophie, was not one she wanted. Nor did marriage seem an option. In her words: "I was the shyest thing and the agony I suffered [meeting gentlemen]."

The spellbinding pull of the natural world and her powerful imagination and talent freed her from the insular and dull destiny of the typical nineteenth-century spinster. The lifelong maiden expressed the sensuous side of herself in her artwork. Her passion for the beautiful in nature helped her transcend the confines of the familiar and build a vibrant life and national reputation. Her most wondrous creation was herself, the Audubon of Wildflowers.

1

CHILDHOOD DAYS

Born in New York, the daughter of parents with deep roots in elite neighborhoods of Brooklyn, Eloise moved to the country when her father, Reverend Lea Luquer, became rector of Saint Matthew's Episcopal Church. She was four. The switch from a bustling city to the bucolic rectory in Bedford changed the course of her life. The natural world would be her focus and wellspring for brilliance.

Family also was essential to her makeup. She always lived with her parents or a sibling. Deeper familial roots—her exceptional American heritage— were much a part of her essence. History became a passionate collaborative interest of all the Luquers and provided lessons in character and obligation. To understand the person who would be honored as the Audubon of Wildflowers, one must begin with family.

If you asked the adult Eloise how she got to the town of Bedford in the first place, the "delightful raconteur," as she was described, might have told you that a bad set of choppers was the reason.

One Sunday, when her father, Lea, was in Manhasset, Long Island, at his parents' country place called the Willows, an old clergyman of the parish broke his false teeth. "He could not read the service," said Eloise as she told the family story in the book of recollections *Old Bedford Days*, "and he sent word to my grandfather to please come and read the evening service." The grandfather, Nicholas Luquer (1810–1864), couldn't do it and sent his son Lea instead. "While he was reading the lesson, a ray of light came through one of the windows, and he had an inspiration that he must study for the church."

Eloise Elizabeth Payne Luquer (1834–1894) and baby Eloise Payne Luquer shared names with aunt Eloise Richards Payne. *The Frick Collection/Frick Art Reference Library Archives.*

The porch of the rectory around 1887. *From left to right*: Delia Marble, Eloise Elizabeth Payne Luquer, Sophie Smith, Sophie Berg, Anne Elizabeth Cottrell Payne, Thatcher T.P. Luquer and Eloise Payne Luquer. *The Frick Collection/Frick Art Reference Library Archives.*

Reverend Lea Luquer (1833–1919) shortly after the move to Bedford in 1866. *The Frick Collection/Frick Art Reference Library Archives.*

Lea, who graduated from Columbia College Law School in 1852, was a practicing attorney at the time, but after being tutored, he was ordained in June 1864, without having set foot in a theological college. (In 1908, Columbia conferred an honorary STD degree, *honoris causa.*) He also was in frail health, so when a pastoral job in the healthier clime of Bedford came his way, he felt that, too, was a sign. "He talked it over with mother," wrote Eloise. "She said she always wanted to marry a lawyer or a clergyman or a farmer, and now she had all three."

On August 12, 1866, Reverend Lea Luquer began his fifty-three-year pastorate at St. Matthew's. "Besides bringing back to the church some of its lost beauty and stateliness," observed a church history, "the Luquer family brought with them to Bedford a merry household of children." The youngest child, Thatcher, was born there soon after the move. Lea McIlvaine, one of the other siblings, was only two, and Eloise was four.

Running this happily busy household could not have been easy. Besides a lack of running water and electricity, the rectory, built in 1811, was drafty and cold. "How Mother got along, I do not know," said Eloise. When wind came from the northwest, "we all had the croup at once. We had a teakettle and they had an umbrella over the teakettle and father would hold one child, mother another."

The needs of parishioners were also high right after the Civil War. The couple averaged four callers a day, plus trips to homes of the sick or forlorn. But the rector had "tremendous concern for people and the desire to make their lives warmer, gentler, and nearer to a living God.…The new rector and the parish were made for each other," said the church history.

The reverend's wife, Eloise Elizabeth, was beloved by all Bedford. She had an "interest in all good works." In the preface to his wife's privately printed book of poetry, Reverend Luquer wrote, "St. Matthew's Parish was brightened by her presence and blessed by her influence."

Another significant member of the family was Eloise's maternal grandmother, Ann Elizabeth Cottrell Payne. As an infant, Eloise and her parents lived in Brooklyn with the Paynes, and then Ann Elizabeth lived

Left: History buffs all, the Luquers gifted museums with items like Grandmother Payne's dress of wool and silk and Grandfather Nicholas Luquer's ten-foot-long family sleigh. *New York Historical Society Quarterly Bulletin.*

Right: An invaluable donation: the portrait of great-great-grandmother Sarah Shippen Lea. Reportedly, Gilbert Stuart said she was the most beautiful woman he ever painted. Her sister Peggy married Benedict Arnold. *National Gallery of Art.*

with the Luquers in the rectory for another twenty-two years. Eloise wrote lovingly of her: "Grandmother was always doing lovely things. She was the sweetest old lady and always wanted to make everybody happy. She was very gentle but always sat. Everybody sat in those days."

Eloise also recalled in *Old Bedford Days* this winter pastime she enjoyed with her grandmother:

> *Then the lovely sleighing! Grandmother had a coupe and two horses. She called them "Rolo" and "Bruno." Every day at three o'clock she would go to Katonah, a long drive of three miles. We were proud to go with her. She always wore a long crepe veil and bonnet. Her dress was bombazine with three rows of crepe around the bottom.*

EARLY LEARNING

The three Luquer children had lessons in the mornings, starting at nine. Their father and mother were undoubtedly skilled teachers. Reverend Luquer had a classical education at Columbia University. Mrs. Luquer's Payne family members were noted educators. Eloise Richards Payne and her sister Anna taught at the famous Berry Academy in Boston, where their

"The female genius" Eloise Richards Payne was acclaimed for her artwork, penmanship and sophisticated letters. Her *belles lettres* are preserved at Harvard. *Undated miniature from The Frick Collection/ Frick Art Reference Library.*

Note the signature roses in the arms of Eloise's muse, Helen "Nellie" Sheldon Jacobs Smillie. Eloise took lessons from Nellie and husband George. *Archives of American Art/Smithsonian Institution.*

father, William, was headmaster in the late colonial period. The sisters later opened "one of the most noticeable schools in America" in Newport, Rhode Island. Their curriculum emphasized visual arts, including drawing from nature, and math, science, drama, languages, moral lessons and elocution. Before practicing law, Thatcher Taylor Payne, Eloise Elizabeth Payne's father, was a teacher and an acting director of a school in Manhattan at the age of just sixteen.

Eloise's brothers were accepted to an exacting boarding school, Trinity Military School at Tivoli-on-Hudson, when they were fourteen. They went on to earn advanced degrees at Columbia: Lea McIlvane Luquer (1864–1930) was granted a doctorate in optical mineralogy in 1894 and taught at the university for two decades, and Thatcher Taylor Payne Luquer (1866–1958) qualified as a mechanical and civil engineer in 1892 and taught for three years at Columbia before joining New York Telephone.

Eloise, after formal lessons with her parents were over for the day, schooled herself in nature. With only a five-year spread in their ages, the three Luquer siblings were built-in playmates. The woody ten acres surrounding the parsonage was the playground where "we rampaged around," said Eloise. The Bedford Garden Club states, "She grew up on the glebe land of the church, surrounded by beautiful woods, meadows, farmlands and a flower garden."

The freedom to explore the acres near St. Matthew's provided Eloise with a deep appreciation of the outdoors. "I have never forgotten the joy of getting out and getting away," she said in her memoir. She estimated finding 265 varieties of wildflowers on the farm and 200 more within five miles. Her delight led to her interest in painting landscapes. "I began by copying pictures in a book—the pump and then a little tree. Father drew very nicely himself and he corrected my work."

Besides tutoring the young Eloise as befitting a Payne, Mrs. Luquer asked her daughter, as she grew older, to accompany her to the city to see "the collections." Eventually, Mrs. Luquer arranged art lessons for her precocious child from landscape artist George Henry Smillie of the Hudson River style. Eloise would take the train to Manhattan, paint there all day and then return home. There were about nine lessons. During one of those lessons, Smillie's wife came in. "I had brought a bunch of flowers for her. She sat down and began to paint the pink roses. I was thrilled. I said, 'That is what I want to do; no more landscapes, I want to paint flowers.'"

2

THE AUDUBON OF WILDFLOWERS

THE YOUNG PAINTER

In her recollections, Eloise said she rejected landscape painting when she began her romance with flowers—but not before she completed eight watercolors of seven historically significant homes on Montauk, Long Island. Her paternal aunt Margaret Shippen Luquer was married to subway developer Alexander Ector Orr, the owner of one of the Montauk summer dwellings known collectively as the Seven Sisters.

What luck for posterity that Eloise, an unspoiled artist in her twenties—with little formal art education to speak of—would be the one picked to capture the Seven Sisters in their own unadorned beginnings. Eloise's watercolors achieved the naturalness and simplicity originally imagined for the places at the end of "The End," as Montauk is nicknamed. The cottages, painted in 1885 before any were expanded or renovated, were thus archived by Eloise while at their truest selves.

The resort Arthur W. Benson established in 1881 "is of profound significance in the development of American landscape architecture, community planning, and architectural design," according to the National Register of Historic Places. Frederick Law Olmsted, the mastermind of Central Park and Prospect Park, "took maximum advantage of vistas and prevailing sea breezes." The architectural firm that Stanford White made famous, McKim, Mead and White, built cottages that are "superb early examples of American 'shingle-style' resort architecture." (See "Gallery," page 65.)

Botanical Art Beginnings

With the Montauk commission successfully completed, Eloise concentrated on what would make her famous. In her amusing, self-deprecating way, she credited her saddlehorse Diana with teaching her the science she would need to create accurate floral representations. "Diana just knew everything. She was a botanist, made me collect all my flowers."

That may be partly true, but Eloise began to seriously study botany and gathered "a sound library on the subject." Then in 1887, when she was twenty-five years old, her father founded chapter 882 of the Agassiz Society. Named for the popular Harvard professor and lecturer Louis Agassiz, the society promoted the study of natural science. Eloise became one of its "most eager members." Her mother was also an enthusiastic and useful original member, serving as president and sometimes secretary until her death in 1894. In one of Mrs. Luquer's reports, she wrote about "taking constant pleasure in the study of the beautiful things in nature." Her daughter would mirror those words in future lectures.

At the age of thirty, Eloise had deep enough knowledge of all manner of plant life that she was elected, in 1892, to the Torrey Botanical Society of New York, thought to be the oldest botanical society in America. In the late 1880s, botany was one of the few sciences open to women. Until the 1840s, the study of botany was "almost exclusively confined to the medical profession, or to a limited number of philosophic minds," according to Jack Kramer, the author of *Women of Flowers: A Tribute to Victorian Women Illustrators*. When it began being considered an appropriate study for women, interest blossomed. None were more interested than Eloise and her friend Delia Marble.

One of Eloise's earliest paintings, circa 1889–1900, *Sanguinaria Canadensis* (bloodroot), appeared in the book *Our Early Wild Flowers*, by Harriet S. Keeler. *Bedford Garden Club.*

DAUGHTER OF THE CHURCH, GUARDIAN OF THE TOWN

During all her life she helped the sick and needy of her parish.
—Bedford Garden Club

Reared by two compassionate parents and a kind maternal grandmother who lived with the family, Eloise felt joy and a sense of duty when giving to others. Sensitive and empathetic, she seemed to have the right words to "cheer the faint of heart," said *A Sesquicentennial History of St. Matthew's Protestant Episcopal Church*. Church members also noticed her fondness for driving in the buggy with her father on parish calls. "This meant travel over country roads at a speed of about four miles an hour, which gave her every chance to study and admire wildflowers," according to *Old Bedford Days*. Her compassion and avocation grew at the same time.

In a letter to philanthropist Helen Clay Frick (1888–1984) in 1953, Bedford local historian Gustavus Kirby (1874–1956) described St. Matthew's when he was a boy.

> *The first pew was occupied by the Luquers; the second by Miss Marble and Delia Marble....On the right hand side the large pew was occupied by the Jays, and I remember old John Jay [John Jay II] very, very well, his son Colonel Jay, and his granddaughter "Moppie" Jay....One of the other large pews was occupied by the Woodcock family and old Mr. Woodcock was slightly deaf and he was always more or less behind in the responses. The Reverend Luquer was a grand minister.*

Kirby's conflated memories date to about 1878, when Eloise's brothers Lea and Thatcher began boarding school. Without her best playmates as distractions, the teenaged Eloise shouldered the serious work of caring for parishioners. She said in her recollections, "By that time I was larger and was doing things around the house, [I] had several families under my wing. One with nine children I had to look after. Anyway I began to do some work."

As a young lady, she took over duties of the Women's Auxiliary of her church. "The Rector's daughter and long a much beloved member of this parish used to bake the communion bread herself," reports the church history. "The altar was covered with a snowy white damask cloth which she alone laundered for the first Sunday of the month."

Another of her church duties was teaching sewing. Miss Jeanie S. Will said, "The Sunday school girls' sewing circle was held around the big dining room table in the rectory on Saturday afternoons. We all looked forward to going to the rectory and had so many pleasant times with our beloved Miss Luquer."

The Red Cross, during both World Wars, benefitted from Eloise's needlework. She was among the founders of the Westchester County Auxiliary No. 20 chapter in 1898. At the Red Cross, she deepened her friendships with the daughters in the Wood family and Delia Marble. This opened the door to community activities beyond the churchyard.

District Nursing Association (DNA)

She brought us the exquisite sympathy and awareness
which were the very breath of her rectory home.
—DNA

The Luquer family and the Wood family of Mount Kisco, like-minded in their intelligent pursuits and devotion to service, established multigenerational friendships with one another. "They sometimes came over on horseback for breakfast," wrote Eloise.

When the oldest child of James and Emily Morris Wood, a Johns Hopkins–trained nurse named Ellen, died of a fever in 1900, Eloise despaired, not only over the loss of her friend but also in concern over losing Ellen's contributions to local nursing. "Father said, 'Don't worry,'" Eloise recalled. "'We will raise a fund to carry on the work.' That was the beginning of the District Nursing." It was the first such organization for rural areas in America.

In 1900 America, the average life expectancy was 47.3 years. In 1916, when the DNA of Westchester set up a clinic-like facility in a home not far from Mount Kisco Railroad Station, it was treating old-timey diseases, such as cholera and diphtheria, and facing newer challenges, such as polio, which was at epidemic levels in New York City. Two years later, the all-woman staffed facility faced the Spanish flu pandemic. What's astonishing from today's perspective is that during these crises, the women aided so many with such meager resources. It wasn't until the 1940s that Eloise could report, "We have ten nurses, ten motors, an ambulance and the hospital."

Eloise committed herself to the DNA from its inception until her death in 1947. Helping her in this endeavor was Delia Marble, who, like Eloise, was on the DNA board for fifty years. Ellen's sister Carolena, a fast friend of Eloise and Delia, chaired the Bedford DNA's important Housing and Nursing committee for two decades. In Eloise's honor, the DNA purchased "a new Ford" for nurses in 1948.

CHARITIES FOR CHILDREN

Not a mother herself, Eloise's maternal instincts were intuitive. An amusing and practical teacher, she knew how to engage schoolchildren and college kids into obtaining "a closer insight into the mysteries and wonders of nature," as she wrote in an Agassiz Society newsletter. In hundreds of appearances, she demonstrated how to sow seeds and make mulch. Her hands-on approach had broad appeal.

Eloise's first efforts to raise money for nonprofits consisted of calls and letter writing. She branched out to coordinate luncheons. Then in the 1930s, the seventy-ish spinster channeled the social skills of her ebullient ancestors, such as her great-grandfather Dominick Lynch, "the most fashionable man of New York," and arranged benefit dances. The Church Mission of Help, the Children's Association and the Society for the Prevention of Cruelty to Children were among the beneficiaries. Often, she was the only single person in attendance. To aid a good cause, she showed up with a great smile and an impressive dress.

BEDFORD FREE LIBRARY

On March 19, 1903, in a room that once was part of Bedford Academy (established in 1809), the Bedford Free Library had its beginnings. Eloise Luquer, Delia Marble and St. Matthew's longtime vestryman and warden William H. Bates had sent an introductory letter to the residents of Bedford containing a detailed proposal for starting a library and requested subscriptions.

Meanwhile, Miss Luquer, her brother Thatcher and the rectory contributed a rug, chairs, bookcases and 500 books from the parish library. By 1912, the volumes totaled 3,258.

The subscription solicitation was a success. But the library continued to run with a sense of frugality. In 1923, when Helen Clay Frick sent in $10 for dues, Eloise wrote her that the fee was $1 and asked if she could give the balance to other organizations, such as Bedford Historical Society. Good at math, Eloise was often appointed treasurer of organizations. She noted total expenses for the first year at $100, which paid the librarian's salary; rent to the Corporation of Bedford Academy, which continued to own the 1807 building; restoration; and maintenance. In 1912, a single light bulb was installed in the library's one room. Central heating replaced a coal stove in 1950, but a telephone and indoor plumbing were not added until the late '50s. Eloise, Thatcher and Delia were members of the library board for the rest of their lives. In 1972, the library building was deeded to the Bedford Historical Society, and the Corporation of Bedford Academy was disbanded. The Rusticus Garden Club and Hopp Ground Garden Club maintain the front gardens, which were redesigned in the fall of 2022.

STONE JUG SCHOOL HOUSE

All members of the Luquer family were lovers and scholars of history. Eloise's program notes and newspaper interviews, for example, mention her membership in National Society of Colonial Dames. Her father and brothers belonged to heritage organizations, such as Holland Society of New York, the Huguenot Society and the General Society of Mayflower Descendants.

Mrs. Luquer was the sole heir of John Howard Payne. Known as America's Hamlet, the actor, playwright and composer was the country's first superstar. In 1823, he wrote the most popular song of the English-speaking world, "Home Sweet Home." Decades later, his fans included President Abraham Lincoln, who had opera singer Adelina Patti perform the song at the White House after the death of his son, Willie; and Queen Victoria, who asked Patti to sing it at Windsor Castle. Charles Dickens, while on a tour of America, said he played the tune on an accordion every night with "a pleasant feeling of sadness." Eloise Elizabeth and her father, Thatcher Payne, met the famous British writer at a dinner party hosted by poet and editor William Cullen Bryant.

This storied past was not lost on Eloise. She viewed preserving history as an honor and a responsibility. Locally, she helped repurpose Bedford Academy as the Bedford Free Library, and when the community outgrew the one-room Stone Jug Schoolhouse, the Agassiz Society, of which Eloise and Delia were members, saw it as the ideal place to install a museum of local history. In 1913, the Bedford Museum was opened and remained in the small stone building until 1970. Owned by the Bedford Historical Society, the "Stone Jug" is now a site museum for nineteenth-century education and is used extensively in the society's educational programs.

BEDFORD HISTORICAL SOCIETY

In 1915, nine local citizens, including Colonel Thatcher Taylor Payne Luquer, Delia Marble and Edith Colgate, rallied together to answer Bedford's first preservation crisis—to save the 1806 Methodist Episcopal church, now known as Historical Hall, which was soon to go up for auction. It was rumored a developer wanted to convert it to a multifamily dwelling. On behalf of this group of nine—five women and four men—Colonel Luquer bid at auction but failed initially to win the bid. An appeal to the new purchaser yielded success, and on February 5, 1916, the Bedford Historical Society was founded to maintain and operate the building as a community house. Eloise assisted her brother in these endeavors. Over the next sixty years, the society acquired six additional buildings for the purpose of preservation, and it cares for the Sutton Clock and Tower and the Bedford 1787 Courthouse and Museum for the benefit of the town.

Besides Historical Hall, the Bedford Free Library and Stone Jug Schoolhouse, the Bedford Historical Society owns and maintains the 1838 Bedford Store as its headquarters, the circa 1838 post office, the

Historical Hall is one of seven properties the Bedford Historical Society oversees. *Bedford Historical Society.*

1906 Lounsbery building and the 1857 Jackson House "that contribute to Bedford's historic character." (See "The Pathway of Eloise and Delia.") In addition to property preservation, the society offers tours, community events and programs that "bring history to life for students young and old."

4

THE ARTIST MATURES

Between 1885 and 1910, Eloise painted more than 213 watercolors of the wildflowers of Westchester County. In total, she executed more than four hundred wildflower studies. Her work was first exhibited in 1910 at the Pratt Institute and later at the National Audubon Society in New York, The Garden Club of America headquarters, the Cooper Union, the Froebel League, the Century Club and at the Annual Exhibition of American Watercolor Society.

As she approached the age of fifty, her work gained even more stature and exposure. Her eight years in the Torrey Society, the exhibit at Pratt and her memberships in the Bedford Garden Club and The Garden Club of America boosted her connections and confidence. Eight of her watercolors were used as illustrations in the 1916 field guide *Our Early Wild Flowers*, written by Cleveland botanist and suffragette Harriet Louise Keller.

The prestigious Fifth Avenue firm Charles Scribner's Sons published *Our Early Wild Flowers*. One of the "Sons," Mount Kisco summer resident Arthur Hawley Scribner, was the president of the company at the time. His wife, Helen Culbertson Annan, a graduate of Bryn Mawr (1891), was the second president of the Bedford Garden Club (1916–17) and a committee member of The Garden Club of America. (See their garden on page 73.)

Art Goes Full Circle to Her First Home: Brooklyn

Although most of Eloise's work depicted the wildflowers of Westchester County, the permanent collection of 212 Luquer art originals—from some of her earliest efforts to her seasoned accomplishments—is housed at the Brooklyn Botanic Gardens (BBG). (See pages 70 and 71.) The family, though devoted to Bedford, always retained close ties with Brooklyn.

Eloise was born in her mother Eloise Elizabeth Payne's family home, 67 First Place, Brooklyn. Eloise Elizabeth and Lea Luquer lived with the Paynes as early as 1860, according to the U.S. census. While Eloise was a baby, Lea served as an Episcopal clergyman at the Church of Atonement at 239 Seventeenth Street, Brooklyn.

The Payne family lived in the borough a relatively short time, though long enough to rate a "colossal" bronze and granite statue for Eloise's noted great-uncle John Howard Payne on the crest of Prospect Park's Sullivan Hill. In 1873, a crowd of more than six thousand attended the unveiling. It's ironic that the monument, vandalized and removed in the 1960s, was originally close to Brooklyn Botanic Garden's new visitor center. East Hampton, New York's Home Sweet Home Museum has the saved bust.

The Paynes' "brief but spectacular moment" in Brooklyn is not comparable to the Luquers' long and esteemed presence. The Luquers' roots date back to a French Huguenot who settled in Bushwick as early as 1658, according to Reverend Lea Luquer's obituary in the *Brooklyn Daily Eagle.* At the time of his death, in 1919, the minister who practiced such thriftiness still had title to a Brooklyn farm that had been in the family for 225 years. He also was kin to the Dutch Middaghs, whose property, according to *Brooklyn Life*, "occupied a considerable part of the Heights." There were other consequential Brooklynites in Eloise's family who had farms (called bouwerys): the Van Couvenhovens, the first European settlers of New Amsterdam (1624) and Flatbush (1636), and the Van der Bilts.

In her memoirs, Eloise recalls an annual New Year's Day party hosted by her widowed paternal grandmother, Sarah Lea Lynch Luquer, at the family mansion on 618 Henry Street, which, before its razing in 1899, was considered a landmark of old South Brooklyn. "Grandmother gave me her engagement bracelet, which I wore on that occasion [her thirteenth birthday]." In the 1890s, when Eloise and her brothers were older, they attended at least three Ihpetonga Balls that the society columns dubbed "Brooklyn's Most Brilliant Social Event." At galas and parties in the borough, Eloise's brother Lea McIlvaine met his future wife, Anne Low Pierrepont, whose lineage was also indelibly linked to Brooklyn. Her father, Henry Evelyn Pierrepont II, was the first president of Brooklyn Academy of Music.

Thus, the Luquer family, lived, worked and were entertained from time to time in a proximity of about 2.6 miles from Brooklyn Botanic Garden in Crown Heights, the repository of Eloise's paintings.

BROOKLYN BOTANIC GARDEN

Much of the Brooklyn Botanic Garden was designed as "a science and learning venue," according to head librarian Kathy Crosby, "though the vista and respite concepts are also important."

As early as 1861, Robert L. Viele, a topographical engineer, in a report to Brooklyn park commissioners, suggested "careful development of indigenous and exotic trees and plants." Half a century later, Norman Taylor was hired as the curator of plants. Like Eloise, he was a member of Torrey Botanical Society and was also well acquainted with Nathaniel Lord Britton and Elizabeth Gertrude Knight (see part II). Britton had hired him as a museum assistant at New York Botanical Garden. Under Taylor's direction (from 1911 to 1929), the first established section at BBG—and the first of its kind in North America—was the native flora section. "The original design featured a woodland and separate wildflower beds, arranged in a systematic grid so that scientists could easily observe and access the plants for research," according to BBG.

"The local or native flora garden was designed to help people recognize and learn about the plants in the area's post glacial habitats, including

The Brooklyn Botanic Garden's visitor center and living roof are located at the 990 Washington Avenue entrance. *Photograph by Blanca Begert for BBG.*

wildflowers," said Crosby. "An experimental economic garden was also in development at the same time in the garden's history. The Children's Garden, more dedicated to growing food and teaching botany, was another early garden, as was the Japanese Garden."

Today, among the BBG's many entrances, the new Steinberg Visitor Center entrance has a living roof, "a mix of mostly native or near native plants," said Crosby. "Lots of grasses, too; a living roof is one way of contributing to the environment." The "green" roof will change throughout the season.

5

THE AUDUBON OF WILDFLOWERS

THE PRESERVATIONIST

Like the man for whom she was nicknamed, John James Audubon, Eloise Luquer, the Audubon of Wildflowers, had a deep concern for conserving her subject matter. The reason behind her effort to help found the Bedford Garden Club (BGC), she said, was to preserve wildflowers. Thus, in 1911, Eloise and her friend Delia Marble signed on as charter members of BGC. A year later, the BGC joined eleven other groups to form The Garden Club of America (GCA). The association was mutually beneficial. The GCA introduced Bedford residents to a fellowship of enthusiasts on a national scale—women "able to carry out its plans, to move collectively and purposefully to accomplishment." And the two Graces proved what Bedford gumption can achieve.

In its very beginnings, in May 1913, the GCA adopted a policy statement that included the aim "to aid in the protection of native plants." The GCA later stated, "The premiere in the effort to save this feature of national beauty was the Wild Flower Preservation Committee and the leading lights of the committee were Delia Marble and Eloise Payne Luquer."

Organized in 1916 and chaired by Delia Marble that year, the Wild Flower Preservation Committee quickly became one of the first GCA committees of national scope. By 1930, when Eloise took the helm, it had evolved into the Conservation Committee (see "Saving the Redwoods of California," on page 40).

As the GCA explained in *A History of Conservation and National Affairs & Legislation*, the original intent "was the simple conservation of what they could immediately see and touch, their gardens and their tangible surroundings." The concept grew to include: "The entire ecosystem of the earth….From one's backyard to the planet: this is the history of conservation within The Garden Club of America and the history of the American conservation movement."

Eloise's art glorified the stunning beauty of native flowers. She also understood and preached the complex role these creations played in sustaining life: nurturing pollinators and thus the food supply, filtering pollutants, controlling erosion and regulating air quality. As one advocate noted: "Wildflowers are as much of the heartbeat of our planet as the oceans."

Eloise's artwork and her mission had perfect synergy: she used her watercolors to illustrate knowledgeable talks on wildflower conservation. Work for garden clubs provided her a multitude of forums to communicate about these twin passions—she gave an estimated twenty thousand presentations in thirty-six states. The BGC bragged on her: "Not only did Miss Luquer know her botany and not only did she paint native wild flowers charmingly and accurately, but above all she had the love of people, the enthusiasm for her subject, the ability to teach, and the most superb sense of humor. These gifts made her always welcome whatever her audience."

Eloise, in the 1937 annual report to GCA, wrote:

> I have spoken this year in many towns and states…showing my paintings and giving my talk about wildflowers. One talk was at Berea College, [Kentucky], and I have found the students much interested in wildflowers, and I helped them to develop a nature trail on a mountain behind the school. I spoke at a Conservation Conference at Laconia, New Hampshire; also to two groups of The Garden Club of America, to the children in the high schools of Mahopac and Peekskill, and to a large group of children at Sparkle Lake; to a branch of the Girl's Friendly Society in Brooklyn; to the Literary Club of Brooklyn and to fourteen groups of Federated Clubs. I have talked to two thousand people, to one thousand children, and three nature trails have been started as a result of telling about our Pound Ridge Trail, sponsored by the Bedford Garden Club. The places I have been to are: Southport, Mahopac, Scarsdale, Hastings, Brooklyn, Bedford Hills, Asheville (North Carolina), Yonkers, Spring Valley…Yorktown Heights, North Bennington (Vermont), Cooperstown, Sparkle Lake, Chappaqua, Saugerties, West Cornwall (Connecticut), Lawrence (Long Island), Nyack, New Haven, (Woman's Club), Mt. Kisco (spoke to the Young Italians), Southport, Shrub Oak (New York), Englewood, Woodridge, New Haven (spoke to the Woman's Club), Pocantico Hills.

The two-volume *The Bedford Garden Club: The Story of the Club* chronicled 1911–55 and 1955–71. *Bedford Garden Club.*

The exhaustive schedule had her on the road for months at a time. Yet, according to listeners, she never seemed fatigued: "She brought a rare common sense and humor which brightened the day whenever she spoke."

Her audiences included not only students and members of garden clubs. One of the groups came from the psychiatric unit at a Westchester County Medical Center. This was the first time nature work had been tried in the occupational therapy course.

As early as 1938, Eloise wrote and illustrated botanical notebooks for the inmates of the women's prison of Westfield State Farm, which would become Bedford Hills Correctional Facility for Women. Luquer's botany lessons and the flower show she initiated at the Co-operative Garden Club on the Hill "sowed the seeds for what would become the prison's much-acclaimed Friendship Garden, the first such community effort to improve the lives of female inmates." The program continued until 1971, according to the Bedford Garden Club.

EAST HAMPTON INFLUENCE

Notes from a garden club meeting held in July 1942 at the Laboratory Theater in East Hampton, New York, offer a sense of Eloise's style of speaking. The event celebrated new nature trails at David Lane.

Eloise had a personal connection to the town. Her great-grandfather William Payne was the first headmaster of Clinton Academy, still a landmark in East Hampton, and her great-uncle John Howard Payne, a composer, lived there. And many of her great-aunts and great-uncles were born there. The following are highlights of the notes:

> *Miss Luquer described her visit to East Hampton at the age of four, when she was brought here for sea bathing. Her bathing suit, described amusingly, is still kept as a family memento. Her talk enthralled her audience, young and old alike.*

Eloise inspired every kind of audience, from inmates to the affluent. Like Eloise, Mrs. William Kissam Vanderbilt (Virginia "Birdie" Fair) (*left*) was an enthusiastic supporter of the Red Cross during World War I and a patron of flowers. Birdie's mansion and famous garden, Rosecliff, is open to visitors in Newport, Rhode Island. Eloise happened to be a Vanderbilt descendant. *Right*: The furred and feathered woman next to Birdie at the 1916 International Flower Show is Martha Cowdin Bacon (Mrs. Robert Bacon), who often appeared at Bedford charity events with her sister Katherine Cowdin Marchand (see part II) and sister-in-law Mrs. Winthrop Cowdin (Lena Potter), original members of the Bedford Garden Club. Martha established a wildflower sanctuary at her estate, Old Acres, in Westbury, Long Island. (See "Gallery" for their gardens.) There are less than six degrees of separation from Martha's relative by marriage Ellen S. Bacon and Eloise. Ellen Bacon bequeathed $50,000 to Eloise. *Library of Congress.*

"Wild flowers," she said, "have been her lifelong hobby; they are always good friends, never go back on you." Her father was for 53 years Rector of Bedford Church. She found 265 varieties of wild flowers growing on their farm in Bedford; and 200 more with the five-mile radius that could be covered by their horse and buggy. These specimens were identified and studied around the one lamp and center table during the quiet evenings.

She traced plant life back to the creation: going from lichens and mosses through the ferns and rushes, stopping to give some hint to the hearers of the pleasures each form of plant life can afford to those who give it time. "Watching mosses come to flower and seed," she said, "give indoor pleasure all through spring." She described the seeding of ferns; up to 100 years ago people used to say that fairies sowed fern seed. She told of rushes that contain mineral, silica, and were formerly used in cleaning silver; and of those rush seeds which explode like fireworks in the warmth of the hand. Describing the evolution of plant life from reeds to trees, Miss Luquer said that "this study re-affirms our faith that human beings too will evolve upward, into something better."

"Instead of pressing flowers in her youth," Miss Luquer said, "she began painting them from life." A representative collection of her wild-flower paintings was shown at the back of the stage as she talked. She spoke of the meaning of plant names, going back to Aristotle's botany of 370 B.C. She pointed out the various families of flowers, and those that should be "enjoyed but not destroyed" and others, very common composite flowers like the daisy and dandelion which may be picked freely. Conservation, she pointed out, is only common sense. "If people really love things, they will want to save them." She described how various wild flowers in this country have come from overseas. She told how plants react to their surroundings.... She ended with a poem:

It doesn't take money, as many suppose,
To enjoy the good things of this earth.
The best of its treasures are free to those
Who know how to value their worth.
The sweetest of music the birds to us sing,
The loveliest flowers grow wild;
The freshest of waters gush out of the spring,
All free to man, woman and child.

An excerpt from another Eloise speech illustrates her charming delivery:

White Clover Leaves at Night.
Trifolium repens

Sleepy-headed clover from *Our Early Wild Flowers*.

Every night, the whole clover family will close up its leaves and go to sleep. The three leaves fall over, making a tent, and it goes to sleep. I told the Girl Scouts once about the clover going to sleep....I saw one girl get up and go out. It was in the evening. She came back in a few moments and said, "They do, they do. I didn't believe you. But the whole field went to sleep." Look at your clover field and you'll be surprised at how sound asleep the plants are.

Saving the Redwoods of California

Eloise and Delia were leaders in the BGC and the GCA from the get-go. Delia was the president of BGC from 1917 to 1919, and Eloise was president from 1933 to 1935. More important to history, Eloise chaired the national conservation committee of the GCA in the crucial years between 1929 and 1932.

In 1930, Eloise and another BGC member, Myra Meyer (see "Gallery," page 75), hopped aboard a private train car to travel from a GCA meeting in Seattle, where Eloise spoke, to the redwood trees in California. Like the other ninety-eight delegates on the trip, the women witnessed widespread logging of the "noblest trees in the world" and vowed with the other convention delegates "to work together for the beauty of our land."

Upon returning home, "These two women (Miss Luquer and Mrs. Charles F. Meyer) were the moving spirits of the whole Idea," reported a BGC journal. "The BGC ably abetted them by raising $4,725 to purchase the first Garden Club of America Redwood Grove of 2,552 acres at Canoe Creek, Humboldt County, California." Of the eighty-nine GCA-affiliated clubs in 1930, Bedford gave the second-largest sum—California gave the largest. The cost of the first grove—the entire watershed of Canoe Creek, two miles on the Redwood Highway—cost $75,000. In 1931, a speaker at the annual Garden Club of America Convention stated:

> *If you will think for just one moment you will realize that you have joined The Garden Club of America because you have wished to look beyond your own garden gates, beyond the highly localized garden club, you have wished to enter a wider sphere and to establish contacts of keener interest.*

Eloise's championing of the redwood grove is "symbolic of this effort to reach out beyond the local realm." The GCA grove in Humboldt Redwoods State Park, California, was formally dedicated in May 1934. The GCA tract now contains more than seventeen groves and 5,100 preserved acres, according to Save the Redwoods League.

NATURE TRAIL AND MUSEUM:
WARD POUND RIDGE RESERVATION

In the early twentieth century, the mass production of bicycles—especially the new designs women could easily ride—and affordable binoculars sparked a heightened interest in nature. By 1925, the timing was right for Westchester County to purchase more than four thousand acres of land in northern Pound Ridge and adjacent Lewisboro to create a park for the growing fans of outdoor activity. Once part of Cortlandt Manor, the original Pound Ridge Reservation had more than thirty farms within its boundaries.

In 1931, the BGC "took an interest in the new park." Eloise Luquer and Delia Marble initiated the idea of a nature trail and museum at Pound Ridge Reservation. They convinced the garden club to hire naturalist and local bird expert William Wheeler to blaze a nature trail and helped mark it themselves. It was one of the first interpretative trails in New York State. The BGC paid Wheeler's salary for three years before the park commission took on this obligation. *The Bedford Garden Club: Story of the Club*, states, "The Club's efforts in terms of time and energy expended by members since then cannot be measured."

The treasurer's reports list almost $20,000 in expenditures until the state stepped in. This was the lion's share of BGC's budget. In 1935, for example, BGC contributed $6,000 for salaries. It demonstrates the generosity of BGC and the persuasive powers of Eloise and Delia.

Overlapping with the Bedford Garden Club's support, from 1933 to 1940, workers from the Works Progress Administration and Civilian Conservation Corps improved roads, built bridges, planted trees and constructed shelters and picnic areas in the park. They also saw to fruition Eloise and Delia's dream of a nature museum, completed in 1937. The museum and its outstanding nature program are some of the firsts of their kind in the United States. Eloise lectured and wrote about nature trails and inspired groups to develop their own:

The Nature Trail follows the brook and is shaded by many fine trees and shrubs. Over 200 plants and trees have been labeled: 20 varieties of ferns are also labeled. We have planted a collection of ferns near the spring so that picnic parties may study them before going through the trail. The path after going by the brook, turns into an open meadow, past some huckleberry bushes and some rocks, so meadow flowers can be found as well as shy flowers that grow among the trees by the brook.

Left: The author's granddaughter Georgia Cameron in the fall of 2022 at Luquer-Marble Memorial Garden at Ward Pound Ridge Reservation. *Author's collection.*

Right: Helen Clay Frick serves cake at an annual picnic at Westmoreland Farm (circa the 1930s). She purchased her home in Bedford around 1920, after her father's death made her the richest single woman in America. *The Frick Collection/Frick Art Reference Library Archives.*

One dream that Eloise and Delia did not live to see come true was a wildflower garden at the reservation. The Bedford Garden Club funded the creation of the garden in 1953–54. Alice Recknagel Ireys, who created the fragrance garden for the blind at the Brooklyn Botanic Garden, was the designer. Helen Clay Frick, a member of the BGC (see "Gallery," page 76) generously supported the memorial garden for her friends Eloise and Delia. Frick also saw to the printing of Eloise's memoir *Old Bedford Days* in 1954 and arranged for one hundred slides to be made of Eloise's artwork.

Today, the Rusticus Garden Club and Bedford Garden Club maintain the wildflower garden. A renovation is underway.

"ALL THE WORLD IS GOD'S OWN FIELD"

In March 1939, the GCA presented Eloise with the medal of achievement for her outstanding work in creating interest in nature and wildflowers.

A decade later, the BGC upped the accolades and established the Eloise Payne Luquer Medal to honor its noteworthy cofounder. It was the first GCA award to have an endowment. The GCA has presented more than forty-five of the medals for special achievement in the field of botany, which may include medical research, fine arts or education.

The Garden Club of America's Eloise Payne Luquer Medal. *The Garden Club of America.*

The prize-winning sculptor Chester Beach, who was well known for his medallic art, was selected as the designer of the award. The motifs on the medal are from Luquer's paintings. The re-creation of her Jack-in-the-pulpit illustration (see "Gallery," page 67) is center stage. The wording "All the world is God's own field" is from a popular Protestant hymn often sung at Thanksgiving, "Come Ye Thankful People Come." In 1844, the composer Henry Alford penned the actual words as "We ourselves are God's own field." He agreed to a revision in 1867: "All the world is God's own field."

Both versions would have suited Miss Luquer. She looked to her own beliefs and skills for the mustard seed of conservation. She envisioned this cause taking root in all the world.

6

THE FINAL YEARS

With the death of their father in 1919, Eloise, then fifty-six, and her brother Thatcher, then fifty-two, moved from the rectory, their home for half a century, to a new home in Bedford Hills. She created a lovely new garden at Rock Meadow. But, said BGC, "she still kept returning to St. Matthew's, not only to continue her life-long interest in the church, but especially to study the grasses and mosses she knew so well on those old acres."

The siblings—their brother Lea, the husband of Anne Low Pierrepont, had died in 1930—continued sharing their mutual interests. Colonel Thatcher Taylor Payne Luquer was one of the five original founders of the Bedford Golf and Tennis Club, and in 1896, he was its very first club champion. His tall (five feet, eight inches), athletic sister was sometimes his golfing partner.

Another cherished joint concern was the District Nursing Association. Eventually, Thatcher was named a director of Northern Westchester Hospital, which evolved from DNA.

The last twenty-eight years of Eloise's life—post–World War I to post–World War II—were certainly not a slowdown for her. In her talks, she outlined her philosophy on aging:

During the winter we think of the plants as just dormant and dead. They're not. They are teaching us the most wonderful lessons of preparedness. All through the fall and the winter they are building their fruit buds and leaves for the next year. Everything is ready now…you realize how everything is being strengthened, every step is a little better—the old is forgotten—the new

Left: Eloise Luquer in a beribboned garden hat. *The Frick Collection/Frick Art Reference Library Archives.*

Right: Colonel Thatcher Taylor Payne Luquer and Eloise Payne Luquer celebrated more than eighty Christmas holidays together. *The Frick Collection/Frick Art Reference Library Archives.*

> *is better—all going ahead....This manifestation of the Creator's power is in all of these steps that we see. And the more we study these flowers the more we realize what they teach us—they teach us patience, they teach us contentment....We are living for the next step—evolution—for ourselves.*

In 1942, at the age of eighty, Eloise—still "going ahead"—employed her efficiency and skills to collect extra gas coupons from the WPA for educational purposes. She gave four talks "at great distances," according to the BGC. That same year, twenty of her wildflower watercolors were exhibited by request at the National Audubon Society in New York. She also was active in the DNA, the BHS, the Red Cross and the Bedford Free Library.

And then, in 1947, it was time for her "next step around the curtain," as she called it. She returned to the earth she so richly appreciated. A resolution of the Bedford Garden Club expresses the deep mourning for this beloved member:

> *Miss Luquer's interests were as diversified as her sympathetic understanding was broad; but with a singleness of purpose she gave unsparingly of herself to whatever responsibility she assumed, bringing to it the full power of her extraordinary mental and social gifts. Her energy was boundless and her attitude toward those with whom she worked typical of her kindness and generosity...*

This pea family is a very interesting family. It is a very ancient and honorable family. The pea has all kinds of characteristics. It has nerves. It has a great many nerves. It is a most sensitive plant. It is sensitive, it is climbing, it is the first family that begins to want to climb up and get high up in the world.

I brought down my baby pea to show you because I thought you would be interested to see. There is a little shoot coming up and there is the little root going down. And it is just six days old. I put it in the cotton garden and the second day it began to grow, and there you see the leaves are starting, the two leaves which will feed the plant. Last time I tried this experiment, my plant lived seven months in cotton wool and water just as well as if I had used soil. And it grew and grew. It grew up over the trellis and then it blossomed.

And so these plants teach us all the time the wonders of creation, and I think that we must just think of that. Think of beautiful things and not of sadness and horrors. I want to say—about the little sensitive plant:

"A sensitive plant in a garden grew.
And the young winds fed it with silver dew
And opened its face like leaves to the light
And closed them beneath the kisses of the night."

—Remarks by E.P.L.; poem by Percy Bysshe Shelley

PART II

DELIA WEST MARBLE

Farmerette Founder

April 6, 1868–June 17, 1951

At ages eleven and five, Eloise Luquer and Delia Marble lived about one and a half miles from each other. Bedford was a small town, and it was a quick buggy ride from the Episcopal parsonage on Cantitoe Street to Marble Farm on the big hill at Old Post Road. For two girls who favored the outdoors as much as Eloise and Delia, a brisk walk cutting through the fields of Woodcock Farm may have been a preferable and fast way to meet up. Their first introduction was perhaps as early as 1873 at St. Matthew's Church, where their family pews were adjacent. For

Teenage Delia, around 1884. *Rippowam Cisqua School.*

the next seventy years, their values and commitments intersected at many meaningful points. Foremost was their appreciation of nature, but they also were united in their concern for rural nursing, conservation, preservation and education.

Unlike Eloise—reared modestly but with the surety of two compassionate parents—Delia was born in an extravagant Fifth Avenue mansion but with a mother for only two months and a father who was, though caring, preoccupied with financial, political and social ambition.

Delia, at about the age of five, moved to Bedford to live with her paternal grandparents and maiden aunt—three educators—while her father, a famous newspaperman and political operative, worked in New York City.

Delia saw enough of her absentee father that his legendary spunk rubbed off on her. Unbound by her grandparents' guardianship in her thirties, the petite, strong-willed woman took off on field trips to the West Indies, Jamaica and Bermuda to identify, catalogue and preserve native plants. Forty of her discoveries became part of the just-beginning New York Botanical Garden.

A decade later, during World War I, she battled the U.S. Departments of Labor and Agriculture to get her way about a woman's land army. She also made the bold personal decision to live with a woman partner. She and her mate, Ida Ogilvie, were leaders of the first successful training camp for farmerettes in America, the Bedford Woman's Agricultural Training Camp.

Because Delia was such a capable champion of the woman's land army, it has become her chief legacy. Much of her story is inseparable from this movement's history, which is also summarized in this biography.

1

CHILDHOOD DAYS

Delia was only two months old in the spring of 1868, when her mother died at the age of thirty-six, leaving two babies—her son Frank was one year old—and a husband, Manton Marble, who also described himself as "orphaned." He wrote, "So to me in the middle of a summer day came out of the sky like the blowing of the resistless winds, whither and or whence I know not, this great bereavement and I am desolate."

Delia Bishop West had been a reliable listener and source of encouragement to Manton. He depended on her to steady his dizzying life as a newspaper publisher and politician.

In 1862, at the age of twenty-seven, career journalist Manton Marble found financing for the newspaper the *New York World* from August Belmont, the husband of Alva Smith Vanderbilt. Manton, as editor from 1860 to 1879, published many of Belmont's views, which he himself embraced. Manton, with Belmont's input, is credited with writing the Democratic platform in 1864. Manton's success propelled him into national prominence and afforded him a "magnificent mansion" on Fifth Avenue. One *World* story that he didn't write about, "400,000 additional draftees," so incensed Republican Abraham Lincoln that the president ordered his arrest. Manton, who was not responsible for the fake news, dodged jail time and prepared a blistering counterattack on President Lincoln. His daughter Delia would inherit his formidable traits *and* his notable kindness.

After his wife's death, a grieving Manton put aside his work, politics and social life. Delia and her brother, born within a year of each other, spent their babyhoods under a cloud of mourning. Then their father chose to lift his sadness and share his paternal duties in an unusual way. He invited his brother-in-law, Cyrus Yale, to move in.

Cyrus had been married to Manton's wife's sister, Martha Kate West. In 1864, Martha had also died soon after giving birth. At some point before 1870, Yale and his three motherless daughters moved into Manton's four-story home at 532 Fifth Avenue. The brownstone became chock-full of children and domestic servants. The comingled houseful of cousins in midtown Manhattan worked for a time. Then a new set of circumstances ushered in change.

Manton Marble (1835–1917) as he appeared in *Harper's Weekly*. *Gilder Lehman Collection, New York.*

To Bedford

The bachelor fathers, Manton and Cyrus, who hobnobbed with other rich and brilliant men of their day, decided on new living arrangements after several years. The misfortunes of the Marble family undoubtedly contributed to the regrouping.

Manton's father, Joel (1803–1887), was a respected public school teacher in Albany, New York. Among his students was his own academically brilliant son Manton, who later graduated from the University of Rochester. But when Joel, in his late fifties, retired from teaching, some slippage began to show in his finances. The 1860 census recorded Joel; wife, Nancy (1810–1898); and daughter Susan (1838–1920) as superintending an orphan asylum in Albany. His personal estate was worth $300.

Manton was well aware of the decline in his family's fortunes. For example, he began paying his brother's tuition. Around 1872, he helped his parents— then sixty-nine and sixty-two—buy a hillside home in Bedford. Five-year-old Delia and her brother, Frank, moved in with their grandparents and aunt on the farm near Cross River Road. For Delia, it would become the place where she thrived. The *New York Sun* reported in 1879, "Here near the farm of Mr. John Jay, Mr. Marble has a fine farm under careful cultivation where he gratifies his taste for good stock, both cattle and horses."

Longtime instructor Joel Marble grew up in the country, and the return to farming was almost welcome, though a professional agrarian, William Jones, also lived on the site. Joel and Manton, mostly still a city dweller, joined the Bedford Farmer's Club, which was organized around 1852. Almost all the men in town belonged to the association, including founders Judge William Jay, Reverend Lea Luquer and James Wood. There were monthly meetings focused on specific agricultural topics or health issues that were pertinent to the community. Sometimes in the summer, a member might host a meeting where he could display a crop or prize cow. Serious business over, they would sit in rockers on the porch, drink lemonade and shoot the breeze. John Jay II entertained the fellows at his home every year.

It's almost certain that Delia, who had a natural affinity for botany and agriculture, trailed her grandfather, the farmer William Jones and sometimes her father as they managed Marble Farm. It is likely she peppered them with questions about the Farmer's Club meetings. She and her friend Carolena Wood, who helped run her own family's place, lobbied to become members. In 1901, as soon as membership was opened to women, they joined. Delia was an officer.

It's also evident that her brother Frank's interest was not in the land but the sea. At the age of seventeen, he enlisted as a cadet at the U.S. Naval Academy and eventually became a commandant in the regular navy. The Marble Farm was destined to be Delia's homestead.

2

YOUNG ADULT

1887–1911

The year 1887 was important to nineteen-year-old Delia. Schooled at home by the three educators in the family and by tutors on occasion, she was ready to branch out in her intellectual pursuits. She joined Chapter 882 of the local Agassiz Society, hosted by Reverend and Mrs. Lea Luquer, where she found rapport with other scholars of natural science and the warmth of a kind-hearted family. With her brother in Annapolis, her father ever busy and her grandfather sinking into death that December, she needed the comfort of the Luquers as much as she needed the distraction of engaging study and lively discourse. Interacting with the group whet her appetite for affiliation and wakened her organizational skills. She became the secretary and later the president of the chapter.

About a decade later, she experienced another year (1897–98) of dread and change. Her father moved with his second wife to Brighton, England. The Spanish-American War began, and Frank, now an officer, was stationed off Cuba and San Juan on the cruiser USS *New York*. Her grandmother Nancy Coes Marble, who had lived with her grandchildren for twenty-five years, died in Bedford at the age of eighty-seven.

Delia worked through her worry and grief by volunteering. The following is one experience she remembered "vividly" around the start of a Red Cross auxiliary, and she wrote about it in *History of the District Nursing Association*:

> *Mrs. Henry Marquand, who was a Cowdin, and Carolena Wood and I happened to be coming up on the train from New York together.....Mrs.*

Landscaper Hutcheson (*center*) also developed gardens for Marchand's sister Mrs. Robert Bacon and sister-in-law Mrs. Winthrop Cowdin. (See page 74.) During World War I, she sponsored farmerettes at her home, Merchiston Farm. *Morris County New Jersey Park Commission.*

Marquand said, "Now look here, we must start a branch of the Red Cross in Westchester County. Will you help?" Of course, we said we would. Mr. Marquand had gone with Teddy Roosevelt's Rough Riders, my brother was in the Navy, and Carolena Wood's sister, who was a trained nurse, was in one of the army hospitals. So we cared enormously....Whatever Mrs. Marquand said to do, that person did, and that was true to the very end of her days.

As Delia's anecdote illustrates, Katherine Cowdin Marquand (1856–1928), the founder of Auxiliary No. 20 of the American Red Cross Relief Committee, modeled charitable behavior and female leadership. "Courage and a personal kindliness…the gift of a vision," a report said of her in 1920.

Delia, in her thirties, was still getting acquainted with her feelings of powerfulness and competency, and she recalled Marquand's authoritativeness in 1898, when the auxiliary was founded. "When Mrs Marquand said, 'You are going to be the secretary and take down the minutes,' I had never done anything like that, and I was more frightened than anyone can imagine."

In later years, Delia would prove as forceful as her guide.

Marquand's other imprint was garden design. Her home, White Gates, landscaped by Martha Brown Hutcheson, was a showplace, and it was a beehive of philanthropic activity. In 1911, Marquand cofounded the Bedford Garden Club. She represented BGC at the first meeting of The Garden Club of America in 1913 and presided over BGC from 1923 to 1925.

DISTRICT NURSING ASSOCIATION (DNA)

As the Spanish-American War wound down, the original Bedford chapter of the Red Cross ended. On November 15, 1898, the District Nursing Association of Northern Westchester began. Mrs. Henry Marquand was president, a position she held for twenty-two years; Miss Eloise Luquer was vice-president; and Miss Delia Marble was secretary. Carolena Wood, according to Delia's history of the DNA, "did the impossible, and enormous work of Director of Nurses for 20 years."

In 1940, at a speech to a DNA meeting, Delia looked back with humor on working with Carolena in the 1890s. Like Katherine Marchand, the Quaker missionary guided Delia on inner courage and confidence: "It was my poor fate," said Delia, "to be put in charge of the little committee to start [other] nursing groups. Miss Carolena Wood unfortunately was with me. She said, when I protested my inanity, 'Nonsense! You can do it perfectly well!' I said, 'I can't get up and tell people what to do.' But she packed me off to start one in White Plains that day."

A DNA *was* established in White Plains and then Scarsdale, New Canaan and Ridgefield. "Inquiries reached us from regions as far distant as Texas and an island off the coast of Maine," reported Marble. Within fifteen years, there were twenty rural DNAs in Westchester County alone. Delia was on the board for fifty years; she was a director (1898–1918) and secretary (1898–1923). She said, "People said it was impossible, that it would be all right in the city but not here in the country. We said, 'It has been done in England.' They replied, 'But they have Florence Nightingale and Queen Victoria, and the Queen provides a pony cart, and they have good roads.' We answered, 'Well, we do not have any Queen Victoria but we will manage.'"

Manage they did. In its initial year, with a starting budget of $250, the DNA collected needed items, such as hot water bags, bedpans, rubber sheets, bandages, towels, diapers, clinical thermometers, soap, bichloride tablets, carbolic and supplies not often recommended in modern nursing, such as spirits of turpentine and mustard leaves. Besides gathering supplies, the ways and means committee organized membership drives, fundraisers and an endowment. The group consulted with Metropolitan and John Hancock Insurance, and the companies agreed to pay visiting nurse fees for policyholders. These revenues, plus contributions from patients who were able to pay, established a solid foundation. The DNA steadily improved local healthcare for decades. As one professional nursing organization put it, "The work was so fine and so practical and so necessary that it grew on its own usefulness." The lone nurse in a horse and buggy developed into ambulance services and the Northern Westchester Hospital.

In 1912, a dozen years after DNA's inception, Carolena Wood, the chair of the nursing and hospital committee, reported its growth:

> *Our nurses have assisted with 106 operations in houses. They have cared for 135 confinement cases.…In emergencies of pneumonia, typhoid, acute indigestion, explosions, burns and the results of the insane Fourth of July our nurses are always fighting a good fight. Nothing is too large or small for them to attempt—from a rapid emergency operation in a little house at night to teaching a patient to sew or crochet that she may have her mind happily employed to aid recovery. Everything that makes for health is our duty.*

When there was need in their community, these undaunted women worked together to fill it, sharing their intelligence, lightheartedness, diligence and unflagging energy. Delia later characterized their cooperative spirit:

> *The first thing for all of you who do not remember back to 1898, is just this: If you have an idea and you are sure it is a good idea, and you can get someone to go along with you, do not pay attention to anyone who says it cannot be done! Just don't consider them! Get the people together and go ahead and do it. We are in an era which we see a great many changes and you must be ready to pick up and go on.*

In this passage, Delia encapsulates the ideals of America's Progressive Era. When a series of inventions—from the zipper and the Crapper to incandescent lighting and elevated water tanks—made everyday life easier, brighter and more comfortable, ordinary citizens started to believe in Progressivism's chief tenet that the human condition could be improved through ingenuity and a collective will. Freed from some very dreary tasks—even buttoning up convoluted clothing was a chore—women, especially, responded to the opportunities and responsibilities of newfound freedoms. They put many of their Victorian constraints, like corsets, away. It was a mass awakening.

At the apex of the Progressive Era, the first decade of the new century, Delia, in her thirties, was a prime candidate for the lure of liberty and action. First and foremost, she had no guardians in place. Her custodial grandparents were gone, her father never returned to America and her aunt Susan, though listed as the head of household in state census records from 1905 to 1915, appeared to have little sway over the strong-minded Delia's decisions—or else she was in lockstep with her niece's wishes. For example, in 1908, Delia and her aunt Susie closed up the farm and wintered in Bermuda.

In 1906, Delia made one of the most independent choices in her life. She traveled to Jamaica with two of the world's most famous botanists to collect specimens.

NEW YORK BOTANICAL GARDEN

Delia took a botany course at Columbia University prior to heading to Jamaica. Her very first field trip was a success. She was given recognition for helping retrieve *Thelypteris brittonae* (slosson ex maxon), a species of maiden fern. The credit in a botanical journal must have given her confidence and a determination to practice what she learned. In late March to early May 1909, when she made a second field trip—this time to Bermuda— her collecting skills showed marked improvement. The New York Botanical Garden (NYBG) listed over two hundred specimens for Miss Marble, and the Brooklyn Botanic Garden listed twelve.

Delia was said to have met Nathaniel Lord Britton, the first director in chief of the New York Botanical Garden, and his wife, botanist/bryologist Elizabeth Knight Britton, through a tutor—or Eloise may have made the introduction. Eloise had known the Brittons since about 1892 through her membership in the Torrey Botanical Club. In 1904, Delia was on the committee for admissions to Torrey.

After their travels together, starting in 1906, Delia became good friends with both Brittons. In 1924, eighteen years after their first trip, Mrs. N. Britton spoke to BGC at Delia's invitation about *Wild Flowers of This District and Their Conservation*. Delia also served as Elizabeth's personal assistant at NYBG, in charge of membership. It's safe to say the association strengthened Delia's knowledge of botany. Her mentor's special interest in wildflowers was also absorbed. While never abandoning mosses, liverworts and ferns, Elizabeth Britton became intrigued with wildflowers, and in 1901–2, she founded the

Nathaniel Lord Britton was the director of the New York Botanical Garden from 1896 to 1929. His wife, Elizabeth, created a wildflower sanctuary at NYBG. *New York Botanical Garden*

Wild Flower Preservation Society of America. (Consider, too, the influence of Delia's friend Eloise's devotion to wildflowers. Eloise submitted local specimens to NYBG and BBG.)

As she entered middle age, Delia felt confident in her vocation and buoyed by her friendships. But another *annus horribilis* was fated.

FRANK LUQUER

Like Eloise Luquer's brothers, Lea and Thatcher, Delia's brother, Frank, attended Trinity Military Institute and graduated with honors. Frank was first in his class and excelled in military science. He secured a place at the U.S. Naval Academy.

The career navy man served in the Spanish-American War of 1898. After reaching the rank of commander, in July 1909, he was assigned a world tour on the *Vermont*. That's when a consequential accident occurred. The *United States Army and Navy Journal and Gazette* reported that he fell down a hatch,

Delia's voyage in 1911 was aboard RMS *Olympic*, the sister ship of two ill-fated vessels: *Titanic* (sunk in 1912) and *Britannica* (sunk in 1916). *Wikimedia Commons.*

"receiving injuries that greatly impaired his health." That November, Frank was assigned to Navy War College in Newport, Rhode Island. Two months later, Delia and her aunt Susan made the trip to Newport to visit him and his wife of six years, Isabel.

When Delia returned for a visit in February 1911, Frank's old wounds were still disabling. They "began to weigh heavily on his mind," the *Gazette* said. On the eve of Valentine's Day, Frank shot himself. *Vulnus sclopeticum*, said his navy records. "The cause which led Commander Marble to commit suicide has been determined and there is to be no further investigation of the matter."

Circumstances dictated that Frank be buried in Newport rather than Bedford. Reverend Lea Luquer broke the news to Frank's aunt Susan.

In England, Frank's father, already saddened by his second wife Abby's death, began to fail. Delia's visit to her father in December 1911 offered needed consolation. Manton's letters between 1911 and 1915 are scant, according to his biographer, George T. McJimsey, but Manton did make note of Delia's visit, and the comments show "the father's love."

3
TRANSITION YEARS

1911–1917

As she did at other vulnerable points in her life, Delia responded to sorrow by reaching out, not burrowing in. A couple of months after her brother's death, nearing her forty-second birthday, she joined a brand-new group that was organizing in town, the Bedford Garden Club (BGC), which was chartered in the spring of 1911. Her experience mirrored Eloise's. It would turn out to be a defining moment. The BGC was training ground for leaders of The Garden Club of America (GCA), which was founded in 1913.

Her confidence as an astute amateur botanist had deepened following her two gainful field trips with the Brittons to Jamaica and Bermuda. In 1913, there were two more trips with her mentors at NYBG—to Puerto Rico and St. Thomas, U.S. Virgin Islands. That same year, she took over as president of the local Agassiz Society. Her seven years of committee work for the Torrey Club and her jobs at NYBG sharpened her organizational savvy. By 1916, Delia was fully prepared to be the first chair of a national committee for GCA: the Wild Flower Preservation Committee. Knowing the subject well and not feeling intimidated by a broader spectrum of peers, Delia "forcefully carried the cause forward," according to *The Story of the Club*. She was chair until 1920. The Bedford Garden Club stated, "June 1916 was the first time the word conservation was used at a meeting. This was the precursor of the valuable Conservation Committee of today."

Delia never neglected her hometown after she assumed national responsibilities. In 1913, as president of the Bedford Agassiz chapter, she flexed some boss lady muscles and won a grant to convert the old Stone Jug Schoolhouse into a town museum, an endeavor she shared with Eloise. She and Eloise also continued on the board of directors of DNA during crucial times: for example, shepherding Pound Ridge through a polio epidemic in 1917. That same year, while chairing a GCA committee, she served as president of the Bedford Garden Club.

To top the year off, in the winter of 1916–17, Delia accepted the invitation to be chairman of the board for Bedford-Rippowam School. Sixteen girls met at the home of Mrs. Cortlandt Van Rensselaer (Georgina Lawrence Wells), a member of BGC. Delia is known as a founding mother of what would become the coeducational Rippowam Cisqua School. She herself, however, had not attended a formal school until she was well into adulthood, and then, only briefly.

THE STARS ALIGN FOR CAMP BEDFORD

SPRING 1917

It is almost mystical the way so many quirky pieces came together to create the country's foremost agricultural training camp for women. America entered World War I on April 2, 1917. Soon after, the New York City Mayor's Committee of Women formed a standing committee on agriculture. A major goal was to recruit women to replace the farmers going off to war. But the women laborers would need training and places to stay close to the fields.

Virginia Gildersleeve, the dean of Barnard College, headed the subgroup and, not finding a teacher of agriculture on her urban campus, asked for help from the professor of another earth subject—geology—Dr. Ida Helen Ogilvie. When a committee chair of The Garden Club of America, Delia Marble, had a meeting with Gildersleeve, the dean suggested she talk to that member of the geology faculty. Delia met Ida. They were together for thirty-four years.

But at this point, a new star enters the story, an Austrian countess (and cue *The Sound of Music*). A Von Trapp family relative, Mrs. Charles Short, had the idea that would solve two roadblocks to training camps: farmers and their wives were wary of providing room and board to young city women, and the women were worried about their personal safety and amusement opportunities in the isolated countryside.

Countess Camilla Hoyos Short, trained in horticulture, had a plan, the unit plan—the women would live together, dorm style, in a central camp and feed and entertain themselves in this supportive, chaperoned environment. Each day, the central unit would divide into work groups and go where they were needed. She knew someone with an abandoned farmhouse in Bedford, where Delia also had a farm, and had connections with others who would donate money and furnishings. When Gildersleeve loaned chauffeurs and cars from Barnard to transport workers and, more importantly, suggested Ida Ogilvie as the camp's dean, the constellation of needs was mostly in place. With incredible focus, brilliant and heretofore underutilized women got it done. Between mid-April, when Gildersleeve's subcommittee first convened, and June 4, when the doors opened, the Bedford Agricultural Training Camp of the Woman's Land Army (WLA) became a reality, a seven-week wonder.

Countess Camilla Hoyos, or Mrs. Charles Short (1880–1953), "looked as if she might have stepped out of some quaint old picture by Reynolds or Goldsborough, with her little white jeweled hands, her grave blue eyes under the broad hat, her slenderness and grace," wrote the *Sun* in July 1917. "It was her experience in England during the first year of the war that made her see the need of getting women into farm work in America before the fields should be too denuded of men."

The Austrian noblewoman was from an intriguing family. Her older sister, Marguerite, was married to Prince Herbert von Bismarck, the son of Germany's "Iron Chancellor" Otto von Bismarck. The chancellor's policies are said to have set the stage for World War I. On her English mother's side of the family, her grandfather Robert Whitehead invented the first effective self-propelled torpedo in 1866. Whitehead left most of his considerable fortune to Camilla's cousin Agathe Whitehead, who was the first wife of Baron Georg von Trapp of *Sound of Music* fame. Camilla and her husband, Charles, had a home in Mount Kisco. *Royalty (Travel) Guide.*

Left: Dean Virginia Gildersleeve was a leader of women in both world wars. In World War II, she and Barnard English instructor Elizabeth Reynard developed WAVES, the women's naval reserve. *Library of Congress.*

Right: In 1946, Gildersleeve and Reynard moved to Bedford. They are buried next to each other at St. Matthew's Cemetery. *Naval History and Heritage Command.*

IDA ENTERS DELIA'S LIFE

The only child of two artists, painter Helen Slade and Hudson River School landscapist John Clinton Ogilvie, Manhattan-born Ida Helen Ogilvie (1874–1963) learned to speak French before she learned to speak English and lived in Europe with her parents from age five to nine. In 1878, the family was back in America, living at 55 West Fifty-Fifth Street. Clinton had a studio at 52 East Twenty-Third Street.

Like Virginia Gildersleeve, Ida attended the Brearley School in Manhattan. In 1900, she graduated from Seven Sister's college Bryn Mawr, where she studied under Florence Bascom, considered the first woman geologist in America.

Inspired by Bascom, Ida earned a PhD in geology from Columbia in 1903 and was appointed the *first* geology teacher at Barnard in 1911. While it was an honor to be the first geology professor at Columbia's sister college, Ida also decided to distinguish herself with a specialty in glacial geology. She cleverly carved out this niche for herself and lectured at both schools. Ogilvie became the first woman to teach a graduate course in geology at a university.

"A daring and intrepid explorer," she investigated glaciation in the Adirondack Mountains, broke trails in the Canadian Rockies and hiked to the very rim of one of the highest volcanoes in Mexico. Her brave pursuit of science was matched with a buoyant spirit. Her classes were popular. A former pupil, in a memorial, said "she took students on field trips in an open car and it was interesting to go on excursions with her as she was a keen observer in the field."

In 1917, the professor, then forty-two, met Delia, then forty-nine. Both were short, according to their passports—Delia was five

Ida Helen Ogilvie, though a specialist in glacial geology, was nevertheless tapped to supervise an agricultural training camp. *Cyclopedia of American Biography.*

feet, two inches tall, and Ida was only two inches taller—but they were imposing figures who lived and worked together for more than three decades.

Ida had learned from her mentor at Bryn Mawr, Florence Bascom, that rock and mineral collections were essential study aids. As their partnership deepened, Ida asked Delia to be curator of the geological samples at Barnard. Delia was also a personal assistant and resolute guardian of the teacher's time. One student recalled Delia saying, "The professor is composing her mind and must not be disturbed!"

GALLERY

THE MONTAUK SEVEN SISTERS

Eloise Luquer's landscape period comprised only the year 1885. Still, the work was significant. These four representative images are courtesy of the East Hampton Library, Long Island Collection.

Developer Arthur Benson's own cottage was one of the most rustic of the Seven Sisters. A friend of the Luquer family, Benson was one of nine individuals who financed the Brooklyn Bridge.

The summer cottage of brothers Henry and Robert Deforest was built in 1883. A porch and brick chimney are common elements in all the Seven Sisters.

Queen Anne styling accents the L-shaped porch of the simply proportioned Andrews House. The second-floor balcony invites sea breezes. The owner was the first librarian of Metropolitan Museum of Art, William Loring Andrews.

The founder of ear and eye hospitals in Brooklyn and Manhattan, ophthalmologist Cornelius R. Agnew, MD, who was a medical director during the Civil War, had a brief period to appreciate the natural vistas of his cottage, which was built in 1884, before his death in 1888.

ELOISE LUQUER'S WILDFLOWER ARTISTRY

Top: Considered Eloise Luquer's signature painting, *Arisaema triphyllum*, Jack-in-the-pulpit, created in 1895, is featured on The Garden Club of America's Eloise Payne Luquer Medal (see chapter 5). *Bedford Garden Club*.

Bottom: *Cornus florida* (flowering dogwood) (1894) shows Eloise's work beyond wildflowers, according to Brooklyn Botanic Garden head librarian Kathy Crosby. *Bedford Garden Club*.

Top: *Papilionaceae*, of the pea family, starred in the Audubon of Wildflowers' talks and lectures. Yellow *Trifolium dubium* (hop clover) is an annual. *Trifolium repens* (white clover) thrives alongside roadsides. *Trifolium pratense* (red clover) is a short-lived perennial. *Bedford Garden Club*.

Bottom: *Sagittaria variabilis* (arrowhead) is an aquatic perennial plant of ponds and streams. It has stout underground rhizomes, which are edible with a high starch content. The Lewis and Clark Expedition ate them in place of bread. *Bedford Garden Club.*

Top: In some paintings, Eloise made striking arrangements of wildflowers. This grouping of four contrasts the long wedge-shape petals of poke milkweed with the smaller-leaved Veronica, a beloved plant for pollinators. Wild pink, in the center, was featured in botanist Elizabeth Britton's pamphlet *Wild Plants Needing Protection*. *Left to right*: *Asclepias exaltata* (poke milkweed), *Silene caroliniana* (wild pink), *Lysimachia punctata* (yellow loosestrife) and *Veronica americana* (speedwell). *Bedford Garden Club.*

Bottom: *Arethusa bulbosa* (calopogon) (*left*) is native and considered rare in some locales. *Habenaria psycodes* (smaller purple fringed orchis) can be found in wet meadows in July and August from Newfoundland to North Carolina and Tennessee. *Bedford Garden Club.*

Above: *Viola papilionacea* (common blue viola) (1893). "Violas mean spring," Eloise said in her speeches. *Brooklyn Botanic Garden*.

Left: *Kalmia latifolia* (American or mountain laurel) (1912). Eloise liked "to lay down a thin translucent wash for background," says Brooklyn Botanic Garden Head Librarian Kathy Crosby. A shadow "added behind/around the plant image" gives the works "a distinctive look." Note the faint writing that spells out the mountain laurel's name. Diane Bamford made substantial contributions to the wildflower research. *Bedford Garden Club*.

Asclepia tuberosa (butterfly weed) (1883) is a "striking orange and the most beautiful of the milkweeds." *Cephalanthus occidentalis* (button bush) has fuzzy white balls. *Asclepias incarnata* (swamp milkweed) "prefers moist marshy places in the sun." *Brooklyn Botanic Garden.*

HISTORIC AMERICAN GARDENS

Enter the private estates of women who featured in the lives of Eloise and Delia. As was true for the two friends, the beauty of flowers and gardens was a refuge in a turbulent age.

Dorothy Claire Conron and her first husband, James Butler Jr., shared this lovely garden. Mrs. Butler won first prize in 1938 at the International Flower Show and also exhibited flower arrangements that same year at the World's Fair. During the 1960s, shop owners, especially those in Bedford Hills, cooperated with the then Mrs. Donald W. Marshall in "far-reaching plans for improving all aspects of the village," according to *The Story of the Club*. These plans included planting trees, window boxes and tubs. *Library of Congress.*

Edith Leonard Colgate, nicknamed "Mrs. Bedford," aided Eloise in supporting the library. She was also a member of the Agassiz Chapter 882, the Red Cross, the DNA, the BHS and a founder of Bedford Garden Club. She had the distinction of being the town's fire commissioner. Frances Benjamin Johnston photographed her garden at Filston Meadows. *Library of Congress.*

Charles Scribner's Sons published *Our Early Wild Flowers* in 1916. One of the "Sons," Mount Kisco summer resident Arthur Hawley Scribner, was the president of the company. His wife, Helen Culbertson Annan, a graduate of Bryn Mawr (1891), was the second president of the Bedford Garden Club (1916–17) and a committee member of The Garden Club of America. The Scribners' Highfields country estate was on Chestnut Ridge Road in Mount Kisco. *Smithsonian Institution, Archives of American Gardens, The Garden Club of America Collection.*

Mrs. Winthrop Cowdin's garden in Bedford. *Library of Congress.*

Martha Cowdin Bacon's wildflower sanctuary in Westbury, Long Island. *Smithsonian Institution, Archives of American Gardens, The Garden Club of America Collection.*

The staircase to the Long Island home of Martha Cowdin Bacon and former U.S. secretary of state and ambassador to France Robert Bacon. *Library of Congress.*

When Myra Comstock Meyer joined Eloise on the trip to California, Myra's husband, Charles F. Meyer, was the president of Standard Oil. The BGC minutes note, "Mrs. Meyer had a charming garden with a lotus pool and Garden of Ease." Her country home was on Highland Avenue in Katonah. *Smithsonian Institution, Archives of American Gardens, The Garden Club of America Collection.*

Georgia Squiers Whitman's Bedford Honour Garden. *Smithsonian Institution Archives of American Gardens, The Garden Club of America Collection.*

A detail from Helen Clay Frick's garden at Westmoreland Farm in Bedford. *Smithsonian Institution Archives of American Gardens, The Garden Club of America Collection.*

Delia West Marble tending her blossoms on Old Post Road. *Smithsonian Institution, Archives of American Gardens, The Garden Club of America Collection.*

Delia's fellow WLA lobbyist Anna Gilman Hill helped fashion Gray Gardens in the Georgica Pond area of East Hampton. *Library of Congress.*

Frances Benjamin Johnston and Mattie Edwards Hewitt photographed Gray Gardens about 1914. *Library of Congress.*

Above: After World War I, actress, producer and activist Bessie Tyree Metcalfe indulged in flowers. This view of Lake Marie was photographed by Frances Benjamin Johnston in 1922. *Library of Congress.*

Left: After a day of gnawing invasive plants, working goats relax in the old barn at Airlie Farm. *Brett Culbreth Mosely Cameron.*

5

BEDFORD GETS ON BOARD

1917

How are we going to feed our Allies across the water and have enough food to feed ourselves?...The crops of 1917 will decide whether the world shall be fed or starve in 1918....For every man who must shoulder a rifle for military duty we had better furnish inducement for another to take up a hoe or farm work.
—New York Times, *March 30, 1917*

Even before America entered the Great War, the farmers of Westchester County had difficulty finding workers. In 1913, former New York City mayor Seth Low, at a meeting of the Bedford Farmers Club at Charles Haines's home, gave a speech, "The Labor Problem." High-paying jobs in factories and men heading off to fight accelerated the shortage. Food scarcity seemed imminent.

Many of the farsighted citizens in and around Bedford were open to the way their neighbors Camilla Short and Delia Marble suggested handling the crisis. Bedford residents were well acquainted with Delia's many years of civic activities—from the Red Cross and DNA to the Bedford Farmers Club and Bedford Garden Club. Her much-admired leadership served her well as she lobbied people throughout the community to accept and support this newest enterprise of training female farmers. The outreach Delia spearheaded was gratifying. She secured the use of Woodcock Farm as the primary residence. Farmerettes "worked a total of 100 local farms, estates and gardens during the inaugural summer," wrote Bedford Hills Historical Museum.

Some of the initial benefactors are mentioned elsewhere in this book: James and Carolena Wood of Braewold Farm; Eloise's sister-in-law and BGC member Mrs. Lea McIlvaine Luquer; Mr. and Mrs. Henry Marquand of White Gates Farm; James and Elizabeth Tyree Metcalfe (see "Gallery," page 80). The following donors also secured Bedford Camp's place in history.

Wilhelmine Dunn Kirby (1885–1941), an officer in BGC, and her husband, **Gustavus Town Kirby** (1874–1956), an early champion of farmerettes, provided work and a cottage for "soldiers of the soil." Their daughter **Wilhelmine K. Kirby** (Mrs. Thomas Waller) (1914–2004) was only a toddler when the farmerettes lived and worked on the family farm. But given her determination, it's likely they rubbed off on her. As an adult, Wilhelmine was active in the Bedford Farmers Club, a president of BGC (1949–51) and a trustee of the Mianus River Gorge Preserve—the Nature Conservancy's first land preservation project. The preserve contains "a rarely surviving remnant of the original primeval forest found by colonial explorers…some of the oldest trees in the United States," according to the Bruce Museum. On a national scale, she was president of the GCA (1965–68), testified before Congress and held a seat on the President's Citizen Advisory Council on Environmental Quality under three presidents, Richard Nixon, Gerald Ford and George H.W. Bush.

Ruth Williams Pruyn Goodrich (1875–1955), an original member of BGC, and her husband, **Colonel David Marvin Goodrich** (1876–1950), provided a tent camp for WLA farmerettes in New Castle. A Rough Rider during the Spanish-American War, Colonel Goodrich remained friends with the Roosevelts, and Alice Roosevelt was a bridesmaid at the Goodriches' wedding. He also served with General Pershing in World War I. After Colonel Goodrich, board chairman of B.F. Goodrich, and Ruth divorced in 1936, he married **Beatrice Morgan Pruyn**, the former wife of Ruth's brother. The second Mrs. Goodrich was an officer in BGC.

Eleanor Jay Iselin (1882–1953) and **Arthur Iselin** (1878–1952), a mercantile banker and polo player, were married in 1905 at New York City's Episcopal St. Agnes Chapel, Reverend Lea Luquer officiating. Eleanor, the only daughter of Colonel William Jay and Lucie Oelrichs, was the last Jay to own the family farm, held for 255 years through seven generations, beginning with America's first chief justice, John Jay. Eleanor was a member of BGC and an officer of DNA. Farmerette Harriet

Geithmann described work on the Jay Homestead in her article "The Woodcock Chronicles" for *Overland Monthly*:

> *Have positively spent the past twenty-four hours eating, drinking, sleeping, milking Susie and weeding out beets in a war garden on the Islan* [Iselin] *estate. 'Tis our second day out working for hire. Up and down, up and down for eight hours we crept on our hands and knees between long rows of mangel beets, weeding with both hands. At noon we flopped down under a horse chestnut tree in a pasture of frisking Shetland ponies, devoured our lunch with a truck driver's keen relish, and were luxuriously at ease with earth and sky and chipmunks....The pulling of weeds in the beet patch seems such worthy work.*

Anne Wroe Scollay Curtis Low (1847–1929), a member of BGC, and her husband, **Seth Low** (1850–1916), retired to Bedford Hills in the 1900s to be close to his Jay and Pierrepont relatives and to their friends, such as the Luquers. Eloise, Thatcher and Lea had known Seth since childhood, and the men cemented their relationship while Seth was president of Columbia University. The two-term Progressive mayor of Brooklyn and one-term mayor of Greater New York was also a partner with their uncle Alexander Orr in creating a rapid transit system. After decades of urban living, Seth appreciated the suburbs. Said to have "played a fair game of golf," he was elected president of Bedford Golf and Tennis Club. His two-hundred-acre Broad Brook Farm on Stone Bridge Lane in Bedford Hills was another compelling interest. He and his wife, Anne, were especially fond of cultivating sweet peas. As in everything he turned his hand to, he garnered top prizes for peas and became president of Bedford Farmer's Cooperative Association. Although Seth died before the launch of the Bedford Camp, he anticipated the shortage of farm labor as early as 1913. Anne, a member of Barnard College's board of trustees and an active supporter of WLA, presented the camp with twenty or so hens for its own use. Harriet Geithmann recalled labor there:

> *Hot as Hades today, but we put in our eight hours on the famous Seth Low estate, picking vegetables....Wore cabbage leaves in the crowns of our hats. It was 106 degrees in the shade, with the prohibitive shade at the other end of the field. We drank water, mopped wildly at our sweating brows, and pulled onions...a chore never to be forgotten.*

Edith Carpenter Macy (1869–1925) and her husband, **V. Everit Macy** (1871–1930), were ever mindful of using their family fortunes (Standard Oil, not the department store) for the benefit of their Westchester community. He was a commissioner of charities and correction, then of public welfare, and at the time of his death, he was the commissioner of parks. The two-hundred-acre V. Everit Macy Park, in Greenburgh, was named in his honor. Edith, a suffragette, was active in the land army movement. She also founded the Westchester County Girl Scout Council. From 1911 to 1925, she chaired Girl Scouts of America's board of directors. We have her to thank for the GSA Camp Edith Macy Training Center and for Girl Scout cookies. Their farm Chilmark, Briarcliff Manor, Scarborough, may have been one of the sites where Girl Scouts and farmerettes worked together.

Girl Scouts still congregate at the Edith Macy Center on Chappaqua Road, Westchester County. *Wikimedia Commons.*

Mabel McAffie Preston (1884–1976) and her children, John and Jean, lived on New Castle farm on Hog Hill Road, while **Lewis Butler Preston** (1876–1922) served in the signal corps in Washington, D.C., during World War I. The family financed a community garden in Bedford Village during this period. Two years after Lewis's death, Mabel married Englishman Sir Edmund V. Gabriel, a colonel during World War I and gentleman usher in the household of King George V (the grandfather of Queen Elizabeth II). Mabel is often referred to as Lady Gabriel in BGC records. Mabel and her daughter, Jean Preston Tilt, both lived into their nineties. Mrs. Tilt's home, Sugar Hill Farm in North Salem, is now the headquarters of Westchester Land Trust, whose staff and volunteers provide fresh, seasonal food to local food banks. The Prestons would have been proud of this modern manifestation of generosity.

Frances Crocker Sloane (1877–1962) and **William Sloane** (1873–1922) carried out an "important enterprise," according to BGC minutes from 1917. During the grape and apple season, "700 pounds of jam and marmalades in ten-pound wooden pails were made and given to Mr. William Sloane for shipment to Y.M.C.A. Canteens overseas." Sloane, the president of the house furnishings company W&J Sloane; his wife, Frances, a BGC member; and their daughter, Margaret, lived during the summers at the 130-acre Merestead ("farmland" in Scottish) at 455 Byram Lake Road, Bedford/Mount Kisco. He chaired the Army and Navy International Committee of the YMCA, and besides supplying farmerette jam to canteens here and abroad, he raised $4 million for the organization. The YMCA's Sloane Houses are named for him. The Sloanes' farm and twenty-eight-room Georgian mansion were donated to Westchester County before their daughter Margaret Sloane Patterson's death in 2000.

Mable Narcissa "Gussie" Cox Vanderlip (1880–1966) and her husband, **Frank Arthur Vanderlip** (1864–1937), established a large dehydrator on their estate for utilizing farmerette produce. Gussie, a University of Chicago graduate and suffragette, was a vice-chair of New York State's Woman's Land Army. Frank Vanderlip was the president of National City Bank (now Citibank) in 1909 and is credited with developing the Federal Reserve System. The couple was married in 1903 and had six children in quick succession. They moved to Scarborough in 1906. By the time children three and four were born, the Vanderlips founded America's first Montessori school in their home, Beechwood, where Frederick Law Olmsted planned the original landscape.

Gussie Vanderlip and three of her children at Beechwood, where Frederick Law Olmsted planned the landscape. Guests at the estate included Annie Oakley, Isadora Duncan and the dancer Vaslav Nijinsky. *Photograph taken in 1919 by Frances Benjamin Johnston and Mattie Edwards Hewitt; Library of Congress.*

MARY SIMPSON MADDOCK AND WOODCOCK FARM

One of the most substantial and necessary contributions to Bedford Camp was Mrs. Maddock's loan of Woodcock Farm for housing. Although some farmerettes quartered at Marble Farm and in tent camps, Woodcock Farm was the primary site. Helen Kennedy Stevens told the *New York Times*:

> *For such a camp as this, the old Woodstock homestead is ideal. With its ample lawns, its high ceilinged and airy rooms, its large barn and its excellent water supply from a picturesque old well, it seems almost to have been planned for the purpose.*
>
> *Here, sleeping in "dorms" in the attic, in sleeping rooms on the second floor or in tents accommodating two occupants, the girls have spent the nights of their happy, busy summer.*

The Woodcocks are believed to have owned the property, which is across the street from what is now Bedford Golf and Tennis Club, as early as the Revolutionary War era. It certainly was in the family when William P. Woodcock (Captain Billy) and his wife, Mary Ann Astor Cook, were listed there in the 1860 census records. Their daughter Mary Ann Astor Woodcock, who never married, resided on the property until her death in May 1908. Her niece Mary Isabella Woodcock Simpson owned land adjacent to the Bedford Country Club. The aunt willed the niece Woodcock Farm, too. Beneficiary Mary Simpson married John Maddock in November 1908. It's unclear if the couple lived in Bedford after their marriage. That's why the house was vacant for a decade *and* available for Mrs. Maddock to loan out. Delia and Camilla Short worked out the agreement. The farmerettes occupied almost every inch of the house for three seasons, more than 160 women in all.

Farmerettes are visible on the porch of Woodcock Farm. *Bedford Historical Society.*

THE WHITMANS AND THE BEDFORD OAK

After the war, in 1919, Harold Cutler Whitman and his wife, Georgia, moved into the Woodcock house "on the road to Bedford," now Cantitoe Street. Georgia Squiers (Squires) Whitman, a member of BGC, chaired an International Flower Show committee. She hosted a viewing of flower arrangements in 1938, and in 1941, her garden was part of a house tour to raise money for the nature trail and the Red Cross. The Whitman place was called Bedford Honour. (See "Gallery," page 76.)

When Georgia died in 1942, Harold Whitman deeded a living treasure and point of pride to the community. The Woodcock-Whitman Oak became the Bedford Oak. The aged tree would be "an object of reverence in any community," wrote L. Hollingsworth Wood in 1952, when the tree was thought to be a mere five hundred hundred years old.

In 1977, Mrs. George C. Sharp, a member of the BGC, and the Bedford Historical Society raised the revenue to protect the tree from nearby development. "The garden clubs all swung into action," wrote the Bedford Historical Society, "the Bedford Garden Club, the Rusticus Club, the Hopp Ground Garden Club and the Green Acres Garden Club all made generous contributions and members were active in the drive."

Before automobiles, citizens tipped their hats as they drove their buggies past the Bedford Oak. *William Abranowicz for the Bedford Historical Society.*

The Bedford Historical Society "owns and maintains two acres which protect the tree from development," according to its website, "and works with the Town's Tree Advisory Board to care for this noble tree and to ensure the preservation of this living monument and cherished symbol to the community."

6

THE CARE AND GROWING
OF FARMERETTES

1917

We were all city girls, enthusiastic but sublimely ignorant of farming.
We all had to be taught several things, among them the difference between a nice
little tomato and a weed. We learned that cows had to be milked at rather regular
intervals and that only hens would lay eggs.
—*Helen Kennedy Stevens,* New York Times

With housing camps and farm work secured, the Bedford Camp was almost ready to train the potential workforce, which publicity and popular culture were rapidly incubating (see chapter 8). How to teach this new breed of women farmers had to be imagined and implemented double-time. The stars once again aligned. Agnes Tisdale Dexter, a Cornell graduate in agriculture who was also certified as a children's garden teacher, was perfectly prepared for instructing the mostly novices. Assisting her from Barnard's geology department was Miss Florrie Holzwasser.

Taking care of home base was on-the-job training for farmerettes. Trade workers and college students alike shared turns in the home garden and dairy that supplied their own food. Chores: planting; weeding; hoeing; harvesting rye, corn, peaches and apples; wielding a scythe; pitching hay. Another undertaking was revitalizing Woodcock Farm, which had been vacant for ten years. Helen Stevens said:

The best fun in the first week was whitewashing the hen house. We had to
ask the grocer boy how to slack the lime, and we found it so exciting that

when we finished the henhouse, we got some more and did the dairy. Then we built a fine chicken yard that would have kept in a herd of buffalo. We cleaned out the stable for the horses and cows that were coming.

Helen Kennedy Stevens became a spokeswoman and recruiter. Testimonials from farmerettes themselves at war-work fairs, articles in popular magazines and brilliant recruitment posters played on the strong patriotism women were already feeling. *From the* New York Times.

One of the chief concerns for Delia, Ida and Dean Gildersleeve was that the women hired needed to stay strong and healthy while performing hard labor. Physician Christine Mann volunteered as a camp doctor that first summer. Nutrition was also a priority. Three "pupil dietitians" from Teachers College, Columbia University, were on hand to cook and plan meals for a hoard of very hungry ladies. They managed to feed fifty women for twenty-five dollars a day—three good meals at fifty cents a head. The frugal meals, calibrated to produce energy for farmhands, comprised fruits, vegetables, eggs, milk and cheeses supplied by the central camp's own two cows, twenty-six hens, vegetable garden and orchard.

Heading the entire kit and caboodle was the dean of Camp Bedford Ida Ogilvie. Some of the recruits already knew the popular dean from Barnard. She was a demanding teacher but seemed equally gifted at earning respect, loyalty and fondness. She chaperoned 11 Barnard students and 140 other farmerettes the first season. Harriet Geithmann said, "When Dr. Ogilvie swung by…I thought of Gibraltor Rock on Mt. Rainier."

Ogilvie's confident, matter-of-fact demeanor also won converts among the townspeople. In the early summer of 1917, seeing 150 girlish newcomers in gingham shirts, overalls and peanut hats may have startled some of the more conservative residents. The *Sun* reported one resident as saying, "If the committee had searched the whole world 'round they couldn't have found a chaperone better equipped to make Westchester swallow overalls for women than Ida H. Ogilvie."

Ogilvie's commanding presence was reassuring to the farmers as well. Under her watch, the women's proficiency and dedication to task grew steadily. The *Westchester Times*, on August 10, 1917, wrote:

At first the farmers treated the idea lightly. Then one or two, finding no available labor, asked for some of the girls. In a week every girl was working outside, and now there is a waiting list of farmers!…The unanimous opinion of the farmers has been that they do more work in a few hours than the ordinary laborer does in a day.

In her article for the *New York Times*, Helen Stephens said the farmerettes, "if they had enough pep," would stop at a swimming hole after work or ride horses. After supper, the girls danced to records on the Victrola. Barnard students recounted fun and woe in the 1920 Mortarboard yearbook: "The evening's spent in song and jest; / The squealing phonograph is going. / She sits and chatters with the rest, / And thinks not of tomorrow's hoeing."

Bedford Ballads, in 1919, says, "I am feeling farmeretty, / Not a single bit regretty.…So I'm as happy as can be / Bossed by Dr. Ogilvie."

NECESSARY OBLIGATION

The plans for the Bedford Agricultural Training Camp for Women were all in place, and from the onset, camp ran smoothly, except for one factor:

In her forty-ninth year, lucky traveler Delia survived a potentially perilous journey to visit her father. On May 23, 1917, she arrived in Liverpool on the USS *St. Louis*, an armed guard for the U.S. Navy. One week later, the same ship dodged a torpedo and struck a submarine. Delia's safe return voyage began on September 1. *From the* Naval Encyclopedia.

Ida's righthand person and partner would not be there for the first growing season. Less than two weeks before the opening, a duty of the heart took precedence. Delia's father was dying. Camp began without her.

7

DELIA'S RETURN

FALL 1917

By the time Delia settled her father's affairs in England and returned home, it was mid-September. Given the speed of steamship travel, she just missed the excitement of the speech at Woodcock Farm on September 15, 1917, from U.S. Department of Agriculture assistant secretary Carl Vrooman. He praised the fifty to sixty "sun-tanned and overall-clad" farmerettes assembled on the lawn, couching his words in 1917 phraseology, "You are a credit to yourselves, to your sex, and to your land."

The crops were in, and there was much to brag about. The experiment of an agricultural training camp was a success in terms of production. Virginia Gildersleeve, on June 13, 1917, said:

> In one day, with several squads working on other estates, the farmerettes put in 22 rows of corn 186 feet long and did the fertilizing. Another day they put in 200 tomato plants, 43 hills of squash and six rows of beans and six of cabbage. And it is on record that the vegetables were in such a hurry to look upon the farmerettes that they broke all Westchester records in coming.

Dean Gildersleeve was pleased that the farmers were happy with the yields and that they were impressed with the summer soldiers' "superior conscientiousness and quickness." She was also relieved that the camp created "a happy, healthy community."

Still, there was much work to be done. First, the next season of workers had to be recruited, and some volunteer staff had to be replaced. Bedford had been envisioned as a model for a full national movement. There was demand for a rollout of new units, but start-up costs ran about $5,000 each. Another reality: even though the workers brought in just less than $5,000 in wages from the farmers, the camp had $10,500 in expenses. The Woman's Land Army needed firmer footing.

No one was more eager than Delia to steady the Bedford Camp. In October, she was appointed chair of The Garden Club of America's War Work Council and the Women's Land Army Farm Unit Plan Committee. She and four other determined women headed to Washington to present a GCA petition to U.S. secretary of labor William B. Wilson.

THE LOBBYISTS

The Garden Club of America laid aside its pleasures and met its duties.
—*Elizabeth Price Martin, first president, The Garden Club of America*

Each of the five Garden Club of America delegates who rendezvoused in the capital in the fall of 1917 had a national reputation, and they represented a powerful constituency of women who were wealthy, "glowing with patriotism" and on the cusp of getting the right to vote. In fact, New York State would grant suffrage to two in the group—Delia and Anna Hill—on November 6, just weeks after the meeting.

Elizabeth Price Martin and her friend **Ernestine Abercrombie Goodman**, "the Joan of Arc of Garden Clubs," organized the Garden Club of Philadelphia in 1904, predating the Bedford Garden Club by seven years. Elizabeth was GCA's first president, and Ernestine was the first secretary and treasurer.

Anna Gilman Hill, a horticulturist and celebrated garden writer, was a director of GCA. Her oceanfront home on Lily Pond Road in Easthampton, purchased in 1913, became famous as Gray Gardens. (See pages 78 and 79.) In 1923, Mrs. Hill was a guest speaker at BGC.

Louisa Yoemans King was a founder of the Garden Club of Michigan and GCA. Called "the fairy godmother of gardening," she was a contributor to *House Beautiful* and *House and Garden* magazines. She wrote ten books on the subject. In 1916, Louisa was a founder and president of the separate organization Women's National Farm and Garden Association (WNF&GA). Its mission was to encourage women to study horticulture, landscape architecture and botany in colleges.

The federal government had not warmed to the idea of a woman's land army, certainly not on the scale that Gildersleeve, Short, Ogilvie, Marble and the GCA leaders had envisioned. President Wilson dismissively suggested that women plant vegetables in between their flowers. The Department of Agriculture, according to Library of Congress historian Ryan Reft, "looked upon the WLA with hostility often belittling its efforts." The three-year-old Department of Labor "eventually would assume authority over the WLA, and displayed something closer to ambivalence."

The fall of 1917 meeting with Secretary Wilson became the first foray in a long battle for recognition. Labor wouldn't pay for a single hoe, tractor, Ford automobile or even a gallon of gas. But the trip to Washington did have symbolic value. The garden club leadership realized the survival of the woman's land army would depend on women themselves.

After the unproductive meeting with Labor Secretary Wilson, Louisa King and horticulturist Hilda Loines, representing WNG&GA, and Delia, representing the GCA, organized a meeting in New York and sent out invitations to the YWCA, women's colleges and training schools, women's clubs, suffrage organizations and an array of state and national bureaus concerned with agriculture and employment.

The women met on December 21, 1917. They decided on a name—the Woman's Land Army of America—and formed an executive committee. Delia chaired the advisory council, Anna Hill was vice-chair and Hilda Loines was the recording secretary. Also on the committee were Louisa King, Ida Ogilvie and Virginia Gildersleeve.

8

SELLING THE FARMERETTES

1917–1918

President Woodrow Wilson was reelected in 1916 on the slogan "He Kept Us Out of War." One year later, he had to rally the country to support an intervention in Europe. The president formed the Committee on Public Information (CPI), which inked twenty thousand newspaper columns a week.

In his book *How We Sold America*, journalist George Creel, the head of CPI, said he recognized right away the importance of creating a division of women's war work. He estimated the division sent 2,305 stories to 19,471 newspapers and women's publications; 292 pictures "showed women actively engaged in war work." Unlike the Departments of Agriculture and Labor, he especially appreciated farmerettes.

Another CPI division, Pictorial Publicity, produced more than 1,400 posters, which, said Creel, could be easily seen and understood. The Mayor's Committee, YWCA, Red Cross and Woman's Land Army developed posters, too. The psychology behind the posters changed as the groups figured out how best to pull the emotional strings that encouraged women to support the war effort. The overall effect of the campaigns was to show women as strong and patriotic at a time when women, especially suffragettes, wanted to project just these characteristics.

Left: One of Ida Ogilvie's geology students at Barnard, Jean E. Mohle, is thought to have been the model for James Montgomery Flagg's *Wake Up, America* poster. *Library of Congress.*

Right: On a couple of occasions, Jean E. Mohle reenacted the ride of Paul Revere. She also foreshadowed street performance artists when she assembled automobile engines in the showroom of a car dealer. *Library of Congress.*

ON BROADWAY

The massive publicity at this watermark period of women's rights and national fervor galvanized farmerette recruiting. The grand success of the call and answer filtered its way into the imaginations of producers, playwrights and composers.

"On paper" the musical *Miss 1917* "had almost everything," wrote a reviewer. Florence Ziegfeld "crammed it with beautiful girls," such as trendsetter and dancer Irene Castle, who had popularized bobbed hair and necklaces worn on the forehead. Guy Bolton and humorist P.G. Wodehouse wrote the book for the musical. Victor Herbert and Jerome Kern, among others, contributed the score. *Miss 1917* was nineteen-year-old rehearsal pianist and pit orchestra conductor George Gershwin's introduction to musical theater. Yet despite, or because of, "almost everything"—acrobats, a performing seal, two trained cows and Harry Kelly and his dog Lizzie—the eighteen scenes were called a "lamentable mishmash." It ran from November 5, 1917, to January 5, 1918.

The second song in act 1 was "The Society Farmerettes." P.G. Wodehouse's lyrics included the verses:

> *Mabel, Mamie, Maude and Lizzie—*
> *Watch the dear things get busy!*
> *Working never makes them dizzy,*
> *Now that they are farmerettes.*
> *Ev'ry day there's something doin:*
> *From the corn the hens they're shooing,*
> *Or the pig requires shampooing,*
> *Now that they are farmerettes.*
> *Ever since they introduced her,*
> *For the farm each girl's a booster:*
> *And her closest friend's the rooster,*
> *Now that she's a farmerette.*

Four months after *Miss 1917* closed, the comedy *Starting Something* premiered. It marked the return to the stage of Bedford Hills resident Bessie Tyree. The one-week run benefitted the Red Cross. The *New York Times*, on May 23, 1918, wrote:

> *FARMERETTE PLAY BY BESSIE TYREE*
> *Girls to the Farm, Boys to the Front, and Audience to the Red Cross.*
>
> *Under inspiration from the Red Cross drive, Mrs. James S. Metcalfe became Bessie Tyree again last night, and for the rest of the week will appear at the French Theatre in Thirty-fifth Street in* Starting Something, *of which she is author and stage manager. It is a "farmerette comedy" in three acts, and it shows how our city girls go back to the land in North Westchester, sending their boys to the front and incidentally inspiring adjacent parts with patriotic fervor.*
>
> *Mrs. Metcalfe is a Westchester farmerette in her own right, and an employer of farmerettes.…The single unveracious detail is the costume of the farmerettes.…Mrs. Metcalfe has arrayed her heroines in the trimmest of knickerbockers with skirted coats. What the play loses in grim, bucolic realism, it gains in decorative quality. The farmerette colony in Bedford Village will please take note.*

Left: Dancer Irene Castle's style in *Miss 1917* predated that of mid-1920s flappers, such as Eloise Brooks and Zelda Fitzgerald. *Mary Evans Picture Gallery.*

Right: James Montgomery Flagg's representative poster of the stage women's group shows an altruist throwing off her scarlet fur-trimmed coat to reveal a white volunteer uniform. (See back cover.) *Library of Congress.*

Elizabeth "Bessie" Tyree was a popular Broadway actress from about 1890 to 1903. She and her husband, James Metcalfe, employed farmerettes at Fenimore (see "Gallery," page 80), their home in Bedford Hills, now part of Bedford Hills Memorial Park. Elizabeth donned overalls and joined them in the field. Also during the Great War, Bessie was a founding member of Stage Women's War Relief Group, which raised more than $7 million through plays and bond rallies for hospital supplies and clothes for soldiers.

Always eager to raise funds for good causes, Bessie Tyree Metcalfe was chair of The Garden Club of America budget committee. In September 1936, according to *The Story of the Club*, her "playlet on the health-properties and histories of vegetables" was "a high point in Bedford Garden Club History." Mrs. Metcalfe had engaged a hillbilly band. "The

This photograph of the founding members demonstrates they hadn't quite abandoned fur-trimmed cloaks for uniforms, as the war relief poster dramatized. Elizabeth Tyree Metcalfe is the third from the right. *New York Public Library/the White Studio.*

cast of vegetables were driven to the stage in a farm wagon filled with straw. As they came in the band struck up 'Nearer My God to Thee' and Mrs. Metcalfe was heard crying out, 'For heaven's sake! Stop those men! I asked them to play 'Turkey in the Straw.'"

9

WINTER WORK, SUMMER HARVEST

1917–1918

As head of the WLAA Advisory Council, Delia was engaged in fine-tuning policies, publicity and logistics with committee members. She also concentrated on the many tasks that needed tending before spring planting. For example, personal notes were needed to sweeten community relations and secure land for the upcoming season. High on her list of contacts was one of the most influential men in town, her friend Carolena Wood's father, James. His endorsement swayed even more farmers to participate, and it was reproduced in national media.

> *Dear Miss Marble (December 5, 1917)*
> *Some eight or ten* [farmers] *who had employed them gave emphatic testimony as to the efficiency of their labor, their marked intelligence, their eagerness to learn the "reason why" of agricultural operations, their zest and steadfastness in their work and their pleasant and unexceptional demeanor....*
>
> *If the expected labor shortage during the coming year is realized there will be an increased demand for such labor....*
> *—James Wood, president, Bedford Farmers Club*

Another priority for Delia was writing to colleges, asking them to enroll farmerettes. The following is a snippet from a typical letter, this one to Vassar:

Let us know what you will be able to do in this great movement to place women on the land.
—Delia Marble, January 10, 1918

The stirring national publicity and grassroots recruiting multiplied the farmerette population in Westchester County. For example, 11 Barnard College students signed on the first year; 150 enlisted for 1918. In all, 434 women enrolled, a 400 percent increase in 1917. Nationally, in 1918, the WLAA signed up 15,000 to 20,000 farmerettes to work in thirty states. Also, the farmers were no longer ambivalent about the women. New York State alone needed 50,0000 more agricultural workers.

Delia and Ida set up the main camp and five satellite units in Bedford. Sometimes, women laborers stayed at Delia's farm. Meeting the national demand would take a great deal more money, but the only revenues thus far came from private donations. The government—staring at worldwide need and headlines trumpeting the WLA's success—would not look beyond old notions of women's roles. Starting with the lobbying trip to Washington in the fall of 1917, Delia, the GCA and other WLA advocates tried but could not even get stamps out of Uncle Sam.

NEW YORK FARMERS BREAK ALL RECORDS
Farmerettes, Tractors and Volunteer Workers Make Up Man-Power Shortage

Heartened by headlines, such as this one from the *New York Times* (September 8, 1918) and the bumper harvest that year, Ida was optimistic when she addressed a state conference of WLA participants in late August 1918. Privately, she and Delia were unsure about the fate of the organization.

That spring, Ida had been a negotiator with state and national agencies and a mix of private organizations, such as the YMCA, the Red Cross, college groups and gardening clubs. Each entity had a different take on the WLA's purpose. Nor were any of the stakeholders, as we would call them today, sure about how much control to cede in exchange for government support—that is, if it could be obtained.

A flurry of activity ensued, as Elaine Weiss carefully details in *Fruits of Victory*. On December 18, 1918, a WLA affiliate agreement was finalized. The WLA was designated a division of the U.S. Employment Service. The women got their stamps, and some salaries were covered. The private sector would still have to do most of the heavy lifting organizing and supplying the camps, with the additional burden of bureaucratic red tape and convoluted oversight. Meanwhile, America's twenty-month involvement in the Great War was wrapping up. Before the government reached an agreement with the WLA, the Armistice was signed on November 11, 1918.

10

NEW PURPOSE

1918–1920

Sitting by the old fireplaces in the double parlor of Airlie Farm, Delia and Ida must have had much to think about that winter of 1918–19. They could see some of their "baby"—the Bedford Camp—through the glass doors overlooking their own victory garden. The dreariness of the sagging vegetables was emblematic.

They had nourished this idea of a woman's land army over two successful seasons. As it grew, they had worked to find it a better home—that is, an organizational structure with a permanent financial foundation. Delia and Ida were, in fact, directors in the new stepchild at labor, the U.S. Employment Service/WLA. (They agreed to honorariums of one dollar per year.) Nevertheless, they must have had inklings of the loss to come. They loved the land army in a way the equivocal authorities in Washington did not. They understood its essence and appeal and its value to women and the country. Ogilvie said, "The Land Army camp is the first institution founded by and for women, for the work women can do, not molded on any preexisting institution for men, not made by men for what they think women need."

Taking stock of the dreams that had been compromised and the challenges ahead, they borrowed from their friend Eloise's philosophy "to go forward" anyhow. As Delia inevitably did when she had a spell of low spirits, she got busier, and Ida was right there with her.

While Delia minded the farm and prepared materials for a newsletter, Ida and writer Helen Kennedy Stevens toured the South by car. They started with the Garden Club of Wilmington, Delaware, on November 12, 1918—the day after the Armistice was signed—then hit the Virginia women's colleges: Mary Baldwin, Randolph Macon, Sweet Briar and Westhampton.

In the interim between Thanksgiving and Christmas, Delia and Ida published their first edition of the *Farmerette,* which stated its mission: "A medium through which the landworkers may keep in touch with each other…and the development and plans of the Land Army.…Its slogan is of the girls by the girls for the girls…stories, camp jokes, tribulations, joys, suggestions."

In mid-January, they attended the national convention of the WLA in Philadelphia and headed west in late January on a lecture tour to invigorate enthusiasm for a woman's land army with a new rationale.

Ida, appointed the WLA's director of recruitment, and Delia attracted good crowds to their speeches in Missouri, Kansas, New Mexico, California, Arizona, Oregon and Washington State. A newsclip in the *Seattle Star* notes an adaptation: "[They are] creating interest in the 'back to the farm' movement for women as a peace proposition."

Post-Armistice, the substance of their speeches and interviews *was* different. Patriotism, labor and food shortages were no longer the primary rationalizations for a woman's land army. Ogilvie told the *Seattle Star*, "The Farmerette has come to stay—not because we must have her, but because she likes it." Ida reiterated the new messaging to the *Seattle Daily Times*: "I believe the lasting enthusiasm the women gain for out-of-doors farm work is the biggest thing in its favor."

A former farmerette reflected: "I found now that as I worked it was usually with a pleasant consciousness of sunlight and good, free air, and there were moments when I paused in my work to take a deep breath and look around the orchard or the field with a sense of wonder."

The last road trip was impressive, but the stars were no longer aligned for a national WLA. With the war over, the patriotic, wealthy, local donors switched to new causes, such as helping the Red Cross and DNA cope with the Spanish flu (spring 1918–summer 1919). Garden clubs, including Delia's, and women's colleges, including Ida's, slowly retreated. Suffragettes, a strong constituency, returned their concentration to the push for women's right to vote—ratified nationally on August 18, 1920. The Employment Service of the Labor Department, in theory, was to help solve some of the money issues, but it had funding deficits of its own, new clients—hundreds of thousands of returning servicemen and unemployed munitions workers—and new political opposition after the Republican sweep in the Congressional midterms of 1918, the so-called Spanish flu pandemic election.

The business model that made the Bedford Agricultural Training Camp a working entity less than two months from its conception was no more. And the directors, according to Weiss, "would soon learn that the federal government was not going to come through with any taxpayer funding at all for the WLA."

The worldwide need for food was more crucial than ever, as Delia, Ida, their Quaker missionary friend Carolena Wood and Herbert Hoover knew full well. Many of the World War I vets would not return to the farm. Ida pointed out to the *Katonah Record*, on April 25, 1919:

> *Much has been said about finding jobs for returning soldiers, and it should be stated that the Land Army wants the soldiers to have the first chance to any job there is. Thus far, however, the boys from over there have not shown any desire to go back on the farm and the need for farmerettes appears to be as great as ever. The Bedford Camp is re-opening in answer to definite requests from the employers and by the advice of the County Farm Agent.*

Food shortages were real—as real as the old problem of labor shortages. But the handwriting was on the wall that women farm workers would not be a solution on a national level. On August 5, 1919, at a meeting in Manhattan, WLA board members, including Delia and Ida, began preparing to dismantle the organization, and voted to dissolve WLA on September 26, 1919. The December 1919 issue of *Farmerette* billed itself as the "honorable discharge issue." The legal dissolution of the WLA corporation occurred on February 2, 1920. Delia and Ida had already moved on from the federal wartime effort, but for years to come, they continued to believe in the peacetime appeal of farmerettes.

The WLA's legacy was lasting.

The *Ladies Home Journal*, in May 1919, stated:

> *The woman has proved herself in the eyes of the nation, and what is equally important and perhaps of more lasting effect, in her own eyes. She has shown her ability to do a man's job, if he allowed it, and to earn a wage approximating a man's wage. She has maintained the industry of the country when, but for her, it must have fallen in ruin.*

Helen E. Buller Smith driving a truck crammed with barrels of milk epitomizes the resolution of farmerettes. *Schlesinger Library, Harvard Radcliffe Institute.*

Ryan Reft of the Library of Congress stated:

> *The WLA…not only helped put food on American tables amidst* [World War I] *but also provided a generation of women with agency and inspiration.…WLA workers would become respected academics, business leaders, and elected officials laying the groundwork for twentieth century feminism.* [As we celebrate the Nineteenth Amendment's one hundredth year], *it seems a good moment to think about how…WLA chapters brought women into the public sphere.*

11

AIRLIE FARM AND MANHATTAN

1920–1940

After the WLA disbanded, Delia and Ida divided their time between an apartment near Barnard College and the farm on weekends. A letter to Helen Clay Frick, inviting her to dinner and a discussion of art treasures of Soviet Russia at the Cosmopolitan Club, features the two addresses, demonstrating the pair's fluidity. It also points to an active social life in both locations and Delia's sustained connection to her treasured friend Eloise. Delia notes, "I am hoping to have Miss Luquer & her brother—you see I am holding out all the attractions I can think of." The penciled writing in the corner is Miss Frick's notation to her secretary to decline. Invitations to and from Helen Frick were reciprocal, however. She was a loyal Bedford friend.

CITY: THE FRICK COLLECTION GALA

Cast your mind to the Christmas season of 1935. The Frick Mansion on Fifth Avenue and Seventieth Street in Manhattan, after two decades of expansion and conversion, was about to open as a public museum. Delia, Eloise and Thatcher Luquer were invited to the formal opening of the Frick Collection on December 11, 1935. On that mild winter afternoon, the museum's sixteen splendid galleries were filled with masterpieces

AIRLIE FARM
BEDFORD
NEW YORK

Address,
49 Claremont Avenue
New York City.

Dear Miss Frick,

Will you dine with me on Sunday evening, Dec. 19th, at the Cosmopolitan Club, at eight o'clock - to meet my brother-in-law, Sir Martin Conway — I do so hope that I can entice you away from Bedford, just this once! — My cousin Mrs Whitman & I are asking some friends to meet him in the evening of that day, in the assembly room of the Club, when he will talk informally on the art treasures of Soviet Russia. It will be so nice if you will join us at dinner; I am hoping to have Miss Luquer & her brother — you see I am holding out all the attractions I can think of, knowing there will be moonlight on the little lake & perhaps fresh snow — but do come.

Sincerely yours
Delia West Marble.

Delia and Eloise frequented the Cosmopolitan Club in Manhattan. *The Frick Collection/Frick Art Reference Library Archives.*

of western painting and an expected mix of such random personalities as Colonel Charles A. and Mrs. Lindbergh, William Randolph Hearst, Mayor F.H. LaGuardia, and the creator of the Gibson girl and his model, Mr. and Mrs. Charles Dana Gibson. It's interesting to imagine that Eloise might have rubbed elbows in the "serene and intimate setting" with invited guest Georgia O'Keeffe, who, like Eloise, created more than two hundred floral images—many, needless to say, on a much larger scale. O'Keeffe painted "big," she once said, "to make even busy New Yorkers take time to see what I see in flowers."

A number of Bedford Garden Club members were asked to the party. Besides Delia and Eloise, two other BGC presidents—founder Mrs. Frank H. Potter and Mrs. Arthur W. Scribner—and future president Wilhelmine Kirby, then age twenty-one, received invitations, as did BGC members Mrs. Lathrop Colgate and Mrs. Gustavus T. Kirby. Others familiar to Delia and Eloise among the seven hundred invitees were Miss Virginia Gildersleeve, Mr. and Mrs. Robert Low Bacon and Mr. and Mrs. Frank A. Vanderlip.

COUNTRY: AIRLIE FARM

Even though they moved between town and country, the place Delia and Ida called home on official documents, such as their passports and census records, was Bedford.

The farm truly was Delia's home now. After settling her father's affairs in 1917, the title to the property, for half a decade made over to August Belmont and Company, belonged to Miss Marble. However, Ida, the much wealthier of the two, must have infused some cash. The name Marble Farm was changed to Airlie Farm, which reflects Ida's paternal family roots—the Scottish Earl of Airlie. Marble Farm was no more.

The 1925 New York State census offers a fuller sense of their lives post–World War I. Delia is listed as the farm manager, Ida as a farmerette, plus there were these workers:

Packard, Marjorie, 26, Farmerette
Morton, Francis, 27, Herdswoman
Bell, Clare M., 34, Gardener
Leiner, Pauline, 80, Chauffeur
Jacomb, Constance, 27, Farmerette
Rippier, Dorothy, 31, Farmerette

In 1929, Ida described the farm to the *Brooklyn Eagle Magazine*. In addition to a wonderful garden, Airlie Farm boasted livestock that included

Top: A sketch of a farmerette in a story about Delia and Ida. "Women," Delia commented, "are recognized experts in animal husbandry." *From the* Brooklyn Eagle *magazine.*

Bottom: The dog girl steers the collie cart. At the bottom of the article, Delia is pictured next to a prized Jersey cow. *From the* Brooklyn Eagle *magazine.*

"50 gold-medaled Jersey cows" on a strict performance schedule of "forty pounds of milk a day and forty pounds of butter fat a month" per cow. Arthur Foster, a land settlement field agent from Oregon, stated, "The two women…know more about Jerseys than anyone in the country."

There were "put out or get out" quotas for five hundred leghorn hens as well as the cows. Perhaps the standards were less strict for the fifty purebred collies—Ida's confessed personal delight. The "dog girl" on the farm taught one of the collies to haul loads in a cart. Cocker spaniels, Percheron horses, Peking ducks, Persian kittens, Shetland ponies and tropical fish were also part of the Airlie menagerie. Delia and Ida were living proof that women could be farmers and relish doing it.

Airlie Farm: Then and Now

This old farmhouse has had many names. In the 1820s, the property was known as Captain Amos Canfield's place, which was mostly handed down through the family until 1870. That's when Manton Marble, Delia's father, purchased it for his aging parents, spinster sister and two motherless children. Manton's mentor August Belmont invested in Marble farm.

Delia and Ida bought out the Belmonts' stake in 1917 and renamed it Airlie Farm. Dort and Betsy Cameron purchased the house and twenty acres in 1982 for their family of six. Today, Dort and Betsy live on the property in a strikingly beautiful, universally accessible cottage designed by their daughter-in-law, architect Kirtley Cameron. Their son Miles, the director of innovation and art teacher at Rippowam Cisqua School; his wife, Brett, an event planner and co-owner of the gifts/home/parties store in Bedford Village, La Maison Fete; and their three children live in the restored old home. The house still retains the dorm-like attic room where some farmerettes lived and vestiges of the old barn. Conservation is a strong family value, and the Camerons are lodging fifty-two working goats at Airlie for a Westchester County–wide green cause. Brett is a member of Bedford Garden Club.

"The unusual architecture of this old farm residence, with a square room on top," gives it "particular character," according to a magazine article. *Brett Culbreth Mosely Cameron.*

BEDFORD TIES

Even during the busy WLA years, Delia never let up on her community responsibilities. Like Eloise, wildflowers and conservation were compelling concerns. Delia was president of Bedford Garden Club in 1918–19, and a chair of the conservation committee from 1931 to 1940. Also like her friend, she chaired the conservation committee for GCA. Delia's terms ran from 1916 to 1920. In 1920, Delia was also on the board of directors of GCA. Together, in 1931, Delia and Eloise developed nature trails at Ward-Pound Ridge Reservation. The wildflower garden there is named for the two friends (see part I).

Since Delia was a young girl, the hillside land near Bedford Village was her comfortable place of belonging. But as she entered her sixties, she and her farming partner Ida considered new horizons. Airlie Farm's then sixty

acres—with its forty prize cows and two bulls, big draft horses, little ponies, clever dogs, prissy cats, busy hens and noisy ducks underfoot—must have begun to seem crowded. In 1930, as Ida contemplated retirement from her academic post at Barnard, the women searched for "wide, beautiful acres."

Recognizing Delia's outstanding work in conservation, The Garden Club of America awarded her the Francis K. Hutchinson Medal in 1943. *The Garden Club of America.*

12

GERMANTOWN

1940–1951

Ida purchased an old one-story house and six hundred acres of good meadow and woodland in Columbia County, New York, on December 4, 1930. The house, built between 1773 and 1784, had once been the home of Peter R. Livingston, a militia colonel during the Revolutionary War. The historic house with a beautiful view was named the Hermitage.

It took nine years to turn the property into a fully equipped dairy farm. Midway through the transformation, fate lent a hand. In August 1935, Helen Slade Ogilvie left her only child, Ida, $3.5 million. The income from the estate financed a renovation of the small house, which included raising the roof and adding a second floor.

Delia, then seventy-one; Ida, then sixty-five; and their friend and former poster girl and Paul Revere reenactor Jean Earl Mohle, then forty-one, were included in the May 1940 census for Bedford. The women and other farmerettes, along with cows, hens and collies, finished transitioning to Columbia County later that year after Ida's retirement as professor emeritus and Delia's as curator at Barnard. Delia, however, held onto Airlie until about 1943.

It is no surprise that the active, sociable women were involved with the historical society in Germantown and were charter members of the Hudson Valley Cocker Spaniel Club. In the summer of 1947, Miss Ida H. Ogilvie and Miss Delia W. Marble hosted a barn dance to benefit the Sail Loft Theaters of Germantown. As was true of Delia's friend Eloise Luquer, they never lost the gift of doing good and having fun.

The renovated Hermitage in Germantown, New York. *House Histree.*

FAREWELL

Delia was a natural curator. In all her many organizations, she was usually the one who took notes, prepared the reports, compiled histories and composed the memorials. When she died at the age of eighty-three in Troy, New York, it was her turn for tributes:

> *A friend who administered both praise and blame fairly, and who always took the large view of our work. She brought us her long remembrances with wit and charm; but she was also very alert to our modern world, eager to the end to share in it and to work in it.*
> *—Bedford Garden Club*

> *The resolution of a few women whose vision combined with knowledge and courage was able to alter the structure and tone of the community.... [She] brought to her task a keen mind, a broad outlook, a deep understanding of its problems and mature judgment. Her wisdom piloted the growing organization through many a struggle for 50 years.*
> *—District Nursing Association*

DELIA W. MARBLE,
A CIVIC LEADER, 83
Upon American entry into World War I Miss Marble helped organize
the first unit of the Women's Land Army of America....A knowledgeable
farmer herself, Miss Marble became Director of Camp Standards of
the Land Army and toured the country with a group organizing units in
various states.
—New York Times, *June 20, 1951*

Delia was buried in Albany Rural Cemetery in Menands, New York. She is in the family plot with her Marble grandparents and her aunt Susan, who died in 1920.

CONCLUSION

THE PATHWAY OF ELOISE AND DELIA

The footprint of these two women can be seen wherever you look in Bedford. Start with the charming village green, established in 1680. Five of the most notable buildings surrounding it have links to the two friends and contribute to Bedford Village's designation as a National Historic District.

In 1903, Eloise Luquer and Delia Marble repurposed the defunct boys' school Bedford Academy into the Bedford Free Library. The small colonial structure at 32 Village Green is still a hub of activity for learners of every age. The Rusticus Garden Club and Hopp Ground Garden Club of Bedford care for the library's seasonal flowers.

Farther to the right of the Green at 11 Pound Ridge Road is the Stone Jug Schoolhouse, built in 1829, and three other landmarks are in view: Bedford Courthouse, the Bedford Store and Historical Hall.

The pathway now heads east along Cantitoe Street to Old Post Road. Up that hill to 751 Old Post Road is Airlie Farm, where Delia lived with her family and, later, Ida Ogilvie. In the period during and about a decade after World War I, some farmerettes bunked down and worked here, too. The record crops that World War I–era women farmers produced helped provision soldiers and citizens alike and won women respect at a time when they were fighting for the right to vote. Some of the farmerettes so relished the autonomy they experienced in working on the land that they continued in agriculture into the 1940s.

Map by Miles Cameron.

1. LIBRARY
2. STONE JUG SCHOOL
3. HISTORICAL HALL
4. BEDFORD STORE
5. COURTHOUSE
6. AIRLIE FARM
7. RIPPOWAM CISQUA
8. BEDFORD OAK
9. WOODCOCK FARM
10. St. MATTHEW'S CHURCH
11. WARD POUND RIDGE

A return to Cantitoe Street brings the route to Rippowam Cisqua School. Delia, considered a "mother" of the school, was chair of its first board of directors a century ago. She would have been proud to know that Ripp, which was girls only during her term, is now coeducational for pre-K through middle school.

Across the street from RCS, the village's signature oak still stretches its elegant limbs on Cantitoe Street and Hook Road. The Bedford Camp farmerettes who lived and trained at Woodcock Farm during the Great War admired the Bedford Oak—then known as the Woodcock Oak—and wrote of its majesty in their journals.

Just a bit farther at 382 Cantitoe Road, Saint Matthew's Episcopal Church, constructed in 1810, continues to nourish parishioners, carrying forward some of the ministries Eloise and her parents established in the mid-1800s.The members of this endearing family, who cared for all the souls of Bedford, are buried in the church's graveyard.

One last stop is less than fifteen minutes away on Route 121 in Cross River: Ward Pound Ridge Reservation. Here, Eloise and Delia helped create one of the first nature trails in America. The native plant garden at the reservation was named in their honor.

The physical trail of Eloise and Delia is less than half an hour's journey by car, about ten miles in length. Not as easily measurable is the imprint of their enduring values. They left their town a legacy of conservation, historical preservation and attention to the entire community's well-being. The villagers of Bedford honor that foundation.

The secret of the women's accomplishments was their understanding of the force of collaboration. Planting "the mustard seed," as Eloise would say. For example, their tiny botany study group sparked an interest in conservation that led to the creation of one of first nature trails in America at Ward Pound Ridge Reservation. It was a model for countless others that Eloise promoted in her speeches nationwide. In another joint effort, the Bedford Garden Club, at the urging of Eloise, Delia and their friends, raised record contributions during the Great Depression. The money was pooled with that of other chapters of The Garden Club of America to purchase a grove of endangered redwoods in California. And without teamwork from the townspeople, Bedford Agricultural Training Camp would not have given rise to farmerettes.

Conservation, respect for history and community well-being continue to be in the air. Bedford's country roads, stone fences, riding trails, farmland and organic markets point to its commitment "to preserving its unique character," wrote historian John Stockbridge. It's noteworthy that within just over six square miles, Bedford can claim ten nature sanctuaries. It is also the site of the Nature Conservancy's first purchase of land and the first National Natural History Landmark, the Mianus River Gorge. L. Hollingsworth Wood said, in 1948, "I like to think that the spirit of these women is caught by newcomers to our community and the urge to help bring better living and more human consideration underlies much of the activity which makes self-indulgence less harmful and generosity more popular."

Delia Marble, who matured in the remarkable turn-of-the-century Progressive Era, summarized the collective will that is the centuries-old underpinning of Bedford: "If you have an idea and you are sure it is a good idea…get the people together and go ahead and do it."

NOTES BY CHAPTER

Part I

Chapter 1

1. L'Equer (L'Esquer): The Luquers descended from Paris-born Jan L'Equer, who arrived aboard the ship *Bruynvis* in New Amsterdam (New York) in June 1658. Five years after landing, French Protestant Jan L'Equer was married in a Dutch church to Rachel, the daughter of Norwegian shipwright and builder Dirk "the Noorman" Volkersten. Dirk was the first recorded European settler in what is now Greenpoint, Brooklyn, and he owned a mile-long frontage on the East River. Dirk's wife's parents, the Vignes, were Walloons, French-speaking Southern Belgians. The Vignes established a farm north of what is now Wall Street, along the East River. Their son Jan Vigne (1624–1689) was the first male child born of Europeans in New Amsterdam. He was Eloise Luquer's sixth-great-uncle. The Vignes were one of the thirty Walloon families selected by the Dutch West India Company to settle in America, according to the New Netherland Institute. They sailed in April 1624, four years after the *Mayflower*.

2. Eloise Luquer's grandfather Nicholas Luquer (1810–1864), "a thin, French-looking man," according to historian Henry Reed Stiles, was part of the sixth generation of Luquers in America. His household at 618 Henry Street in Brooklyn included seven English and Irish servants, one of whom was a coachman who probably drove the sleigh that was later donated to the

New York Historical Society. Built about 1830, the sleigh "is both capacious and graceful in line," according to the society's quarterly bulletin. "There are four seats; a high one for the driver, which makes a back for the low seat just behind it; a low high-backed seat in the rear; and in the middle a high seat that is removable....With the sleigh came two large buffalo robes, one of them the gift of Mrs. Lea McIlvaine Luquer."

3. Sarah Shippen Lea's original portrait was painted around 1795. First donated to Corcoran Gallery of Art in Washington, D.C., it's now at National Gallery of Art.

4. Thatcher Taylor Payne: The youngest of nine children in a brilliant yet self-described "turbulent" family, Eloise Elizabeth Payne's father needed to mature quickly, and he did. Orphaned at age sixteen, the teenager felt compelled to step in as director of his father William's academy in New York City. He and his sisters Anna and Eloise opened a new school at 346 Broadway, in what is now Tribeca. Thatcher then taught at Madame Chegaray's Boarding and Day School for Young Ladies, one of the most prominent and tony schools for women in the country. In 1913, he studied at a law office while teaching. "I receive $1,000 per annum, which, with what little remains of Eloises's business, keeps our heads above the waters of despair," he wrote to his brother John Howard Payne. His law practice became financially successful.

5. George Smillie and his wife, Helen "Nellie" Sheldon Jacobs, shared a studio in Manhattan. Eloise also took lessons from her. Mrs. Smillie's portrait is from 1887.

Chapter 2

1. Arthur Benson, a Luquer family friend, was one of nine individuals who financed the Brooklyn Bridge. His city home abutted the Brooklyn Heights Promenade.

2. Eloise's aunt Margaret and uncle Alexander Orr owned a house that stood in the easternmost point in the Montauk Association. In 1924, it was purchased by Harrison Tweed and nicknamed Tick House. An accidental fire burned it down in 1997. Eloise's original watercolor has not been found. Orr made a bequest to Eloise in his will.

3. The Agassiz Association, founded in 1875, "was designed to be an extended free school of natural science," according to its handbook. Over time, there were some fees for the home study. Delia Marble, the Bedford

chapter secretary upon the death of Mrs. Luquer, stated that "nine of us have joined in taking the admirable courses on botany offered by Mr. Wight, those on ferns, trees and composite having been selected."

Chapter 3

1. John Jay, America's first chief justice, took a leading role in the founding of St. Matthew's Episcopal Church. He advanced $2,500 to purchase the land. The construction of the church began in 1807, and it's reported that Jay bore "more than half the cost." St. Matthew's records state that Jay also donated the pulpit Bible, and his daughter Maria Banyer was probably the donor of a silver communion service. The Jays continued their loyalty to St. Matthew's over the next four generations. The family "trooped off every Sunday morning dutifully to worship at St. Matthew's Episcopal Church," wrote Stephen Birmingham in *America's Secret Aristocracy*. There were reminders of "the family's long prominence in the region: stained-glass windows, pews, altar decorations, a reredos, all benefactions from the Jays." Many members of the family are interred in the Jay vault in the churchyard.

Reverend Lea Luquer was well acquainted with John Jay's grandson John Jay II and his great-grandson Colonel William Jay. Both Jays were wardens at St. Matthew's. All three men graduated from Columbia College and thus were entitled to membership in the stylish men's club in New York City the Century Association. They were also members of the Huguenot Society, the organization of French Protestant descendants. John Jay II founded a chapter in his Manhattan home in 1883. Colonel William and Reverend Lea were officers together from as early as 1888 to about 1903, and their common interest in ancestry groups also included the Dutch-related St. Nicholas Society. Reverend Luquer participated in the Episcopal burial services for John Jay II at Trinity Chapel in New York City and conducted the graveside service in Bedford. On a happier occasion, in 1904, Reverend Luquer assisted in officiating at wedding services at New York's Episcopal Saint Agnes Chapel when William's only daughter, Eleanor, married Arthur Iselin. After the funeral for Colonel William Jay at Trinity Church in New York, Reverend Dr. Lea Luquer, the colonel's friend for almost fifty years, said goodbye at the graveside service he led at Bedford.

2. Lea McIlvaine Luquer and Thatcher Taylor Payne Luquer were also active in heritage organizations. Lea McIlvaine Luquer served for five years as secretary of the Huguenot Society. The brothers were also members of

male-only Saint Nicholas Society, which "preserves knowledge of the history and customs of New York City's Dutch forebears." Thatcher was a governor. Both were leaders in the New York Society of Mayflower Descendants. Their ancestors William Brewster, Constance Hopkins and Stephen Hopkins were aboard the *Mayflower*. Stephen Hopkins was also a Jamestowne settler, according to the Jamestowne Society, "and survivor of the wreck of the *Sea Venture*, reputed to be the basis for Shakespeare's comedy *The Tempest*." Lea M. and Thatcher were officers of New York Society of Colonial Wars, for which they completed applications for six ancestors.

3. James Wood was the town supervisor of Bedford for many years. He and his wife, Emily Hollingsworth Morris, and their three children, Ellen, L. Hollingsworth and Carolena, fulfilled their Quaker religious beliefs through deeds of mercy. Carolena chaired Bedford DNA's important Housing and Nursing Committee for two decades.

4. Dominick Lynch Jr., Eloise Luquer's great-grandfather, was first known as a gifted talker while he was a student at Georgetown University; he recited the elegy in 1799 to mourn the death of President Washington, a friend of his father's. Before he turned forty, Lynch was living on Greenwich Street in Manhattan and was the acknowledged social leader "and most fashionable man of New York." According to *The Old Merchants of New York City*, Dominick, who was the director of a bank and sold his own brand of Chateau Margaux, "coined money and spent it with the freedom of a prince. He was a high liver, gave royal dinners, and went into the best society." An enthusiastic patron of the arts, he arranged a concert with the celebrated Garcia Troupe, part of the first Italian opera season in New York City. He left "no fortune to his daughters," however, including Eloise's grandmother. His great-great-grandchildren donated his portrait to the New York Historical Society. Dominick Lynch Sr. was a founder of Georgetown University and Manhattan's St. Peter's Church.

5. Colonel Thatcher Taylor Payne Luquer was the founder of the Bedford Historical Society; president of the Westchester County Historical Society; director of Boscobel Inc., a committee to preserve the Historic Boscobel Mansion at Crugers on Hudson; director of Northern Westchester Hospital. On September 8, 1915, Thatcher Taylor Payne reported for training in New York. His rank was corporal. Almost forty-nine, he was nineteen years older than the draft age, and war was not officially declared until December 17, 1917. But duty, as this amateur genealogist knew all too well, was part of his family's makeup. He rose through the ranks in quick order—corporal to captain to major and, finally, lieutenant colonel at age fifty-one. He

arrived at Le Havre, France, on August 8, 1918. On October 5, he became commanding officer of 306th engineers, which was engaged in the vicinity of Verdun and advancing toward Metz until the armistice on November 11, 1918. He received a citation on December 25, 1918, "for gallant and meritorious conduct and for signal ability and skill in the Engineer Regiment during its recent operations."

6. Edith Leonard Colgate, nicknamed "Mrs. Bedford," aided Eloise in supporting the library and was a lifetime board member. She was also a member of the Agassiz Chapter 882, so important to Eloise and Delia. Other ways she featured in their circle of friends included being a founder of Bedford Garden Club and a member of the Wildflower Committee. In addition, she joined the Red Cross, the DNA and had the distinction of being the town's fire commissioner. She played a central role in the founding of the Bedford Historical Society.

Chapter 4

1. John Howard Payne, Eloise Elizabeth Payne's bachelor uncle, traveled to London at the age of twenty-two and stayed abroad for twenty years, building his career as a playwright, poet and actor. Indeed, his renditions of the Prince of Denmark character were so singular that he gained the sobriquet of America's Hamlet. Famously impecunious, the celebrated composer and actor was in and out of money scrapes and once landed in London's Fleet Prison for his debts. "I cannot reconcile my plans to my means," he wrote to his sister Eloise Payne in 1817. More than a century later, his grandnephew Thatcher T. Payne Luquer edited *Writing a Play in Debtor's Prison: Extracts from the Diary of John Howard Payne, Author of* Home Sweet Home. Scribner's published the edited diary in 1921.

In the 1830s, having returned to the United States, the rootless John Howard lived for a while in New York with his brother Thatcher Taylor Payne and his family. Eloise Luquer's mother, Eloise Elizabeth, was a baby at the time. John Howard stayed with them again in 1848. The niece and uncle had an ongoing affectionate relationship. She was his sole heir. On June 9, 1883, John Howard Payne, who had died in Tunis nearly fifty years earlier, was reinterred in Oak Hill Cemetery in Washington, D.C. Financier William Corcoran, who, as a boy, had watched him perform, paid for the actor's body to be exhumed and shipped to New York. After Payne's body lay in state at New York's City Hall, a special railroad car transported it to the nation's capital. The full U.S. Marine Band, led by John Philip Sousa, played before the audience of two thousand in attendance, according to eyewitness Gabriel Harrison. Congress was adjourned to attend the funeral. The stately procession accompanying the coffin included foreign diplomats, members of the cabinet and Supreme Court and U.S. president Chester A. Arthur. In the heart of it all, between the pallbearers and the president, were John Howard Payne's relatives—Reverend and Mrs. Luquer of Bedford Station, New York.

2. Jan Aertszen Van de Bilt, Eloise Luquer's sixth-great-grandfather, was the first Vanderbilt in America, arriving in 1650 from the village of De Bilt in Utrecht, Netherlands. His farm on the south side of Clarkson Avenue is now part of Prospect Park, Brooklyn.

Chapter 5

1. Martha Cowdin Bacon, the sister of Katherine Cowdin Marquand, married Robert Bacon, the U.S. secretary of state under Theodore Roosevelt and the U.S. ambassador to France (1909–12) under President William Howard Taft. Martha Brookes Brown Hutcheson designed their gardens in Old Westbury, Long Island.

2. Virginia Fair Vanderbilt was a "silver heiress" in her own right. Her father, Henry, discovered the Comstock Lode.

3. In 1962, the Bedford Garden Club honored Frick with a medal of merit "for presenting 105 acres to form the Westmoreland Sanctuary."

Part II

Chapter 1

1. Manton Marble wrote the Democratic platform in 1864 and chaired the National Democratic Committee that year. Twenty years later, he was still in charge of writing the party's credo. The article that incensed President Lincoln was a hoax the *Brooklyn Eagle* perpetuated. It was a forged presidential proclamation. The "night editors allowed it to slip by," according to Manton's biographer George T. McJimsey. Perhaps Marble was distracted. His marriage to Delia West in Rochester was planned for May 19, 1864. The

news was out on May 18. Marble "personally rushed to the docks to reclaim outbound copies of *New York World*, but the orders remained in force." Joseph Pulitzer purchased the struggling paper in 1883.

Marble dined frequently at Delmonico's, patronized the opera and entertained at the mansion that his friend philosopher John Fiske described as "magnificent." A member of the male-only Century Association, which also had as members the Luquer men, Manton cofounded the Manhattan Club with one of the paper's backers, August Belmont. His Fifth Avenue mansion mate and brother-in-law Cyrus Yale was treasurer. Manton had a term as president. The Manhattan cocktail was first served at the club at a banquet held to honor Samuel J. Tilden, a presidential candidate Marble strongly supported. Manton had promoted Tilden's successful election bid as New York's twenty-fifth governor.

Chapter 2

1. Katherine Cowdin Marquand was "a prominent charity worker in New York and Washington and former president of Noel House, the settlement house of Northeast Washington," according to her obituary. Mrs. Marquand's second husband, Henry, a newspaper writer/editor and prison reformer, was the son of financier and art collector Henry Gurdon Marquand, the second president of the Metropolitan Museum of Art. The elder Marquand is credited with acquiring the museum's earliest collection of old master Flemish, Dutch, French and Italian paintings, including Vermeer's *Young Woman with a Water Pitcher*. Henry and Katherine's country home in Bedford Hills was the setting for charitable fundraising musicales, lawn parties and teas and meetings of the Bedford Farmers Club and Bedford Garden Club. One of their fêtes to benefit DNA attracted two thousand attendees. The *Katonah Record* of July 1920 chattily previewed the gala. "It is going to be the most thrilling event of the sort ever seen in this neighborhood. The great feature is to be a Fashion Pageant in which two hundred people are to take part.…Mrs. James S. Metcalfe…has the enthusiastic co-operation of all the pretty girls and good looking men in the district."
2. Winthrop Cowdin, the brother of Katherine Marquand and Martha Bacon, married Lena T. Potter. Their summer home was Newcastle House in Mount Kisco.

Chapter 4

1. Virginia C. Gildersleeve (1877–1965) lived with her parents on West Forty-Eighth Street off Fifth Avenue until their deaths in 1923. After graduating from the all-girls Brearley School in 1895, she enrolled in Barnard College, at that time only three blocks from her home. She was class president. In 1911, Dr. Gildersleeve became dean of Barnard, a post she held thirty-six years. At her direction, Barnard supplied the Woman's Land Army with personnel, including a bookkeeper and drivers, and paved the way for students to become farmerettes.

2. Elizabeth Reynard, who met Gildersleeve while she was an English instructor at Barnard, was the first woman lieutenant in the U.S. Navy Reserves.

3. Camilla Hoyos Short "formed an advisory panel of Westchester neighbors, coaxing them to pledge $5,000 to equip and run the camp," wrote Elaine F. Weiss in *Fruits of Victory: The Woman's Land Army of America in the Great War.* "One supporter offered a farmhouse for the women to live in while others provided cots, chairs and tableware to furnish it." The book *Bedford Garden Club: The Story of the Club* attributes the securing of Woodcock Farm to Delia Marble.

4. John Clinton Ogilvie (1838–1900), born into a wealthy, established New York family, was able to study landscape painting in Switzerland, Paris and at the French Riviera. His wife, Helen Slade (1851–1935), reportedly distraught at his death in 1900, funded Bishop's House, now called Ogilvie House, and the deanery of St. John the Divine in his memory.

Chapter 5

1. Wilhelmine Kirby was often referred to as "the Grand Dame of Bedford," according to a memorial by Abby Luby. She had a deep love and understanding of the land and protecting it. In *Silent Spring*, scientist Rachel Carson wrote about Wilhelmine's struggle to force agricultural officials to stop spraying her property with DDT. According to the *Record Review*, "She would go into the trenches at planning board meetings.…It was so much fun to watch the developers' faces."

2. Harold Whitman later married Edna Jardine Fortington, the daughter of an English baron, in 1945. Edna's first husband, Harold A. Fortington, was a chairman of Paramount Pictures. The second Mrs. Whitman was a member of BGC.

The Whitmans' youngest daughter, Josefa "Fefa" Whitman Myer, recalled living on Woodcock Farm between the Great Wars. She later helped farm the property. "Seven British girls and I harvested the crops.…We worked from seven-thirty in the morning until five in the afternoon."

During World War II, according to *Bedford Garden Club: The Story of the Club* the Whitmans' two older daughters, Bedford Garden Club members Misses Georgia Mary and Helen Morton Whitman, "produced 55 tons of vegetables on their 40-acre Tool Shed Farm.…It is hard to visualize the stupendous scope of the work done under and by these two indefatigable women."

3. SavATree conducted a study of the white oak on Route 22 and Hook Road a decade ago, according to an article by Eric Gendron in the July 21, 2013 edition of *Daily Voice Bedford*. The Bedford Oak was "more than 30 feet thick at its biggest girth and its branches spread more than 120 feet from tip to tip." The tree's age is still an estimate.

Chapter 8

1. Jean E. Mohle, a Paul Revere reenactor, according to the 1940 U.S. census, lived with her mother in Bedford, near Myra Meyer. Jean Mohle moved that same year to Germantown with Delia and Ida.

2. Tony Ring and Christopher Bellew of the P.G. Woodhouse Society granted permission "to spread sweetness and light," according to Ring's email. "Now you can publish his lyrics and sing them with abandon in the shower," added Bellew.

3. James Metcalfe, the husband of actress Bessie Tyree, was a drama critic whose acerbic wit was legendary. In 1905, the managers of forty-seven theaters in greater New York voted to exclude him from entering their theaters. On the other hand, he had a reputation for being markedly charitable. In 1918, he was awarded the Legion of Honor at the highest rank of chevalier for his work with French orphans. James and Bessie lived at Finemore.

GALLERY

1. Dorothy Claire Conron (1897–1991) was active in the Bedford Garden Club during her three marriages. In 1948, after marrying her second

husband, Albert Hunt Marckwald, she was an exhibitions chair of BGC and earned a third prize at the International Flower Show. In 1961, she was a chair of BGC's Fiftieth Anniversary Party. By then, she was married to her third husband, Bedford's town historian for twenty-five years, Donald W. Marshall. The Garden Club of America recognized her leadership, "creative vision, perseverance and enthusiasm" with the Medal of Merit in 1966. She was a cochair of The Garden Club of America Zone III meeting in 1967. The mother of Dorothy's daughter-in-law Jessie Ewing (Mrs. James Butler III), Mrs. William Ewing of Broad Brook Road, and daughter-in-law Anne Gaughan (Mrs. Pierce J. Butler) of Middle Patent Road were engaged in BGC activities as well.

2. Myra Comstock Meyer was Bedford's correspondent for GCA in 1927 and 1928. In 1925, Myra addressed BGC with a lecture titled "Gardens of the Far East." She and her husband had traveled extensively in the Far East.

BIBLIOGRAPHY

Ancestry.com. www.ancestry.com. Census records, passports, photographs, newspaper items and other historical material.

Barbour, Hugh. *Quaker Crosscurrents: Three Hundred Years of Friends in the New York Yearly Meetings*. Syracuse, NY: Syracuse University Press, 1995.

———. "The Woods of Mt. Kisco." *Quaker History* 87, no. 1 (Spring 1988): 1–34.

Barnard Archives online. https://archives.barnard.edu and https://digitalcollections.barnard.edu.

Bedford Free Library. "About the Bedford Free Library/History." https://www.bedfordfreelibrary.org.

Bedford Garden Club. Letter, excerpts from Luquer-Marble lectures on labeling plants for nature trails and paying the salary of William Wheeler. May 23, 1936.

———. "The Story of the Club 1955–1971." Katonah, NY: Katonah Publishing Corp., 1971. www.thebgc.org/bgc-histories.html.

Bedford Hills Historical Museum. *Farmerettes Exhibit*. 2009. www.BHHM.pdf.

Bianco, Shirley Lindefjeld, and John Stockbridge. Images of America: *Bedford*. Charleston, SC: Arcadia Publishing, 2002.

Billy Rose Theatre Division, New York Public Library. "Stage Women's War Relief Founding Members." New York Public Library Digital Collections. 1915–1919. https://digitalcollections.nypl.org/items/5ad85910-9585-0135-d213-4bbecccac12c.

Boston Herald. "Miss Bacon's Will Gives to Charity." October 9, 1924.

Brainard, Charles H. *John Howard Payne: A Biographical Sketch.* Washington, D.C.: George A. Coolidge, 1885.

Britton, Elizabeth. *Wild Plants Needing Protection.* New York: New York Botanical Garden, 1912.

Brooklyn Daily Eagle. "Historic Families United." December 1, 1896. (Marriage announcement of Lea M. Luquer and Anne Low Pierrepont at Grace Episcopal Church, which her grandparents cofounded.)

———. "The Ihpetonga Ball." 1890, 1892, 1893, 1894, 1898. (Guest lists.)

———. "Woman Professor Runs Farm." August 4, 1929.

Brooklyn Eagle Magazine. "Farming Beats Business as an Occupation for Women." February 1, 1931.

Brooklyn Historical Society. "Guide to the Luquer and Payne Families Papers." https://www.bklynlibrary.org. (Now the Center for Brooklyn History at Brooklyn Public Library.)

———. "Guide to the Nicholas Covenhoven Papers." https://www.bklynlibrary.org. (Now the Center for Brooklyn History at Brooklyn Public Library.)

Brooklyn Life. Alexander Ector Orr obituary. 1914.

———. Lea M. Luquer and Anne Pierrepont wedding announcement. September 5, 1896.

Buchman, Lisa. "America's First Green Girls: Bedford Garden Club Centennial 1911–2011." May 27, 2011. www.patch.com.

Cameron, Mable Ward. *The Biographical Cyclopedia of American Women.* N.p.: Halvord, 1924. www.onlinebooks.library.upenn.edu.

"Countess Camilla Hoyos to Wed." *Navy and Army Illustrated* 8 (August 21, 1912): 325. www.royalmusingsblogspot.com/2012/08.

Creel, George. *How We Advertised America.* New York: Harper and Brothers, 1920.

Crosby, Kathy. "Luquer's Lesson." Notes on Power Point presentation of Brooklyn Botanic Garden's head librarian titled "Nature's Counsel: Botanical Art by Eloise Payne Luquer," as reported by Charlotte Tancin. www.BBG.org

Cultural Landscape Foundation. "Alice Recknagel Ireys." Cultural Landscape Foundation. www.tclf.org.

Delafield, John Ross. *Yearbook of the Dutchess County Historical Society.* New York: Dutchess County Historical Society, 1939.

Encyclopaedia Brittanica. "Elizabeth Gertrude Knight Britton: American Botanist." www. Brittanica.com.

Estersohn, Peter. "The Hermitage: Linlithgo, Columbia County, New York." In *Life Along the Hudson: The Historic Country Estates of the Livingston Family.* New York: Rizzoli, 2018. www.househistree.com

Fiftieth Anniversary of the Rectorship of the Rev. Lea Luquer, S.J.D. Bedford, NY: St. Matthew's Church, August 12, 1916.

Find a Grave. "Gussie Mable 'Narcissa' Cox Vanderlip." www.findagrave.com.

Fitch, Charles. *Encyclopedia of Biography of New York.* Reprint, London: Forgotten Books, 2018.

Frick Collection, Frick Art Reference Library Archives. Six images of the Luquer family; letter of Gustavus Kirby; letter to Helen Frick from Eloise Luquer; photograph of Helen Clay Frick at Westmoreland Farm; letter to Helen Frick from Delia Marble.

Garden Club of America Bulletin (January 1923).

Garden Club of America Collection/Archives of American Gardens, Smithsonian Institution.

Gendron, Eric. "Study Finds Bedford's 500-Year-Old Oak Tree in Good Health." *Daily Voice Bedford*, October 2, 2013. www.dailyvoice.com/new-york/bedford/lifestyle.

George Grantham Bain Collection, Library of Congress. Photograph of Mrs. William Kissam Vanderbilt and Martha Waldron Cowdin Bacon at the International Flower Show; Stage Women's War Relief poster; photograph of Jean Mohle.

Gildersleeve, Virginia. "Women on the Land." A report published by The Woman's Land Army of America. New York. April 1918.

———. Report on Woman's Land Army. June 13, 1917.

Gillespie, Samuel. *History of Clay County, Iowa.* Chicago: S.J. Clarke Publishing Company, 1909. (Information on Squiers and Woodcock families.)

Griffin, Ernest Freeland. *Westchester County and Its People.* Vol. 2. New York: Lewis Historical Publishing Company, 1946.

Harrison, Gabriel. *John Howard Payne: Dramatist, Poet, Actor and Author of Home, Sweet Home!* Philadelphia: J.B. Lippincott & Co., 1885.

"History of the District Nursing Association of Northern Westchester Based on an account by Delia W. Marble and on annual reports and surveys." Mount Kisco, NY: Merritt Print Inc., 1948.

Inquirer. "Stroudsburg Hotels Report Big Bookings." June 21, 1913. (Barnard College guests included Ida. H. Ogilvie, Florence Holzwasser and Jean E. Mohle.)

Katonah Record. "Women's Agricultural Camp Praised by Secretary Vrooman." April 25, 1919. (Interview with Ida Ogilvie.)

Keller, Harriet S. *Our Early Wildflowers*. New York: Charles Scribner's Sons, 1916.

Kerr, Adelaide. "Bostonian, 43, Cited for World War I Activity: Lieut. Elizabeth Reynard Helped Lay Groundwork for Women's Naval Unit." *News Journal*, August 29, 1942.

Kerr, Paul F. "Memorial of Lea McIvaine. Luquer." *American Mineralogist*, no. 3 (1931): 97–98.

Kramer, Jack. *Women of Flowers: A Tribute to Victorian Women Illustrators*. New York: Stewart, Tabori & Chang, 1996.

Luby, Abby. "Grand Dame of Bedford, Steward of Guard Hill, Wilhelmine Stewart Kirby Waller Is Dead at Age 90." *Record Review*, April 2004. www.abbylubby.com.

Luquer, Eloise. "Bedford Garden Club Has Trail at Pound Ridge." *New Castle Tribune*, April 5, 1935.

———. *Old Bedford Days: Recollections of Eloise Payne Luquer*. Bedford Village, NY: Privately printed by Helen Clay Frick, 1953.

Luquer, Eloise Elizabeth. *The Poems of Eloise Elizabeth Luquer*. Privately printed, 1894. Whitefish, MT: Kessinger's Rare Reprints, 2008.

Luquer, Lea. *Minerals in Rock Sections*. New York: D. Van Norstrand Co., 1898.

Lynch family. *American Catholic Researches* 5, no. 2 (April 1888): 73–78.

Marble, Delia. "84th Annual Meeting of Bedford Farmers' Club." *Katonah Record*, April 3, 1936. (Memories of Carolena Wood.)

———. Letter Delia Marble to Hollingsworth Wood about Farmers Club. April 25, 1948.

Marquand, Katherine. "Address of the President." *District Nursing Association Newsletter*, n.p.

McJimsey, George T. *Genteel Partisan: Manton Marble, 1834–1917*. Ames: Iowa State University Press, 1971.

Meade, Helen Rutherford. *Bedford Garden Club: The Story of the Club 1911–1955*. Kingsport, TN: Kingsport Press, 1955. www.thebgc.org/bgc-histories.html.

———. *The Story of the Bedford Garden Club, 1911–1955*. Clinchfield, TN: Kingsport Press, 1955.

Myer, Fefa Whitman. "Victory Garden." *Bedford Historical Society Stories* 30 (November 18, 2015).

National Women's History Museum. Posters of farmerettes.

New Castle News. "Resolution Given on Miss Marble." July 6, 1951.

New York Botanical Garden. "Wild Flower Preservation Society of America Records. 1894–1960." www.library.nybg.org

New York Botanical Garden Archives. "Collections Were Made by Miss Delia Marble March 29–May 3, 1909." Series 1 correspondence. Folder 3.78. 1883–1932.

New York Daily News. "Millionaire Balks Pursuing Wife, 2 Nations in Wilds." July 4, 1941. ("For seven months she and daughter Nadia have been unable to catch up with Fortington to serve him with a New York Supreme Court separation and divorce order.")

New York Herald Tribune. Complete list of those invited to the 1935 reception. December 12, 1935. www.frick.org.

———. "List of Guests Invited to the Formal Opening of the Frick Art Collection." December 12, 1935.

New York Public Library Digital Collections. "Stage Women's War Relief Founding Members." Billy Rose Theatre Division Scrapbook. The White Studio.

New York Sun. "Mr. Manton Marble's Marriage." July 10, 1879.

New York Times. "Delia W. Marble, a Civic Leader, 83." June 20, 1951.

———. "Farmerette Play by Bessie Tyree." May 23, 1918.

———. "Mrs. Ogilvie's Will to Benefit Hospital; St. Luke's Destined to Get Residuary Estate After Death of Daughter." August 30, 1935.

New York Tribune. "Miss Pierrepont Becomes Mrs. Lea McIlvaine Luquer—Both Families Well Known in Brooklyn." December 1896.

O'Keeffe, Georgia. Passage originally published in exhibition catalog *An American Place.*

Orinda Garden Club. "A History of Conservation and National Affairs & Legislation, The Garden Club of America 1913–2013." www.orindagc.org.

Poughkeepsie Journal. "Miss Ogilvie Hostess to Summer Players." August 26, 1947. (Ogilvie and Marble charter members of the Hudson Valley Cocker Spaniel Club, April 4, 1946.)

Reft, Ryan. "World War I: The Womens Land Army." Library of Congress. March 26, 2018. www.blogs.loc.gov/loc/2018/03/world-war-i-the-womens-land-army.

Sabine, Lillian. "Woman Professor Runs Farm." *Brooklyn Eagle*, August 4, 1949.

Seale, William. *The Garden Club of America: One Hundred Years of a Growing Legacy.* Washington, D.C.: Smithsonian Books, 2013.

Seattle Star. "Farmerette Campaigner." March 19, 1919.

Seattle Sunday Times. "Seek Recruits for Land Army." March 16, 1919. (Photographs by White of New York City.)

A Sesquicentennial History of St. Matthew's Protestant Episcopal Church. N.p.: Private printing, 1960. By members of the parish family.

Shaw, Martin. "Farming Beats Business as an Occupation for Women." *Brooklyn Eagle Magazine*, February 1, 1931.

"Sleigh Built for Nicholas Luquer, of Brooklyn, About 1830." *New York Historical Society Quarterly Bulletin* (April 1932): 5, 29, 56. (Presented in April 1932 by Miss Eloise P. Luquer and Colonel Thatcher T.P. Luquer.)

Standard Union. "Noted Engineer: Was Member of Old Brooklyn Family." January 31, 1930.

Stevens, Helen Kennedy. "City Girl to Farm Worker: Her Own Story." *New York Times*, February 24, 1918.

Stiles, Henry Reed. *A History of the City of Brooklyn*. Vol. 2. Published by subscription, 1869. Onlinebooks.library.upenn.edu.

Stuart, Gilbert. *Portrait of Sarah Shippen Lea*. National Gallery of Art. Public domain.

Torrey Society. Standing Committee on Admissions. January 27, 1904.

United States Army and Navy Journal and Gazette. New York: U.S. Spanish-American War Military and Naval Service Record, 1911.

Vincent, Roger. *Dare to Be True: A History of the Rippowam Cisqua School: The First Seventy-Five Years*. Dexter, MI: Thomson-Shore Printing, January 1, 1995.

Watters, Sam. *Gardens for a Beautiful America 1895–1935*. Brooklyn, NY: Acanthus Press, 2012. Published in collaboration with the Library of Congress.

Weiss, Elaine. *Fruits of Victory: The Woman's Land Army of America in the Great War*. Washington, D.C.: Potomac Press, 2008.

Westchester County and Its People, a Record. New York: Lewis Historical Publishing Company, 1946.

Westchester County Historical Society Bulletin. "In Memoriam Col. Thatcher Taylor Payne Luquer." N.p.

———. "In Memoriam Miss Eloise Payne Luquer." N.p.

———. "In Memoriam Mrs. Anne Pierrepont Luquer." N.p.

Westchester Times. August 10, 1917. (A report on one of the farmers of Bedford accepting women laborers.)

Wikipedia. "Louisa Boyd Yeomans King." www.wikipedia.com.

———. "Macy, V. Everit." www.wikipedia.com.

Williams, Gray. *Picturing Our Past: National Register Sites in Westchester County*. New York: Westchester County Historical Society, 2003.

Wilson, James Grant. *Appletons' Cyclopedia of American Biography*. Vol. 4. *Clinton Halsey Ogilvie*. New York: D. Appleton and Co., 1887.

———. *Appletons' Cyclopedia of American Biography*. Vol. 4. *Ida Helen Ogilvie*. Edited by James E. Homans. New York: D. Appleton and Co., 1887.

Wood, Elizabeth A. "Memorial to Ida Helen Ogilvie (1874–1963)." *Geological Society of America Bulletin* 75, no. 2 (February 1964).

Wood, L. Hollingsworth. Remarks to Croton Valley Meeting on the death of his sister, Carolena.

"The Woodstock Chronicles." *Overland Monthly*, n.p.

ABOUT THE AUTHOR

Stephen Savage.

After being named a *Glamour* magazine "Top 10 College Girl" in 1972, Judy Culbreth moved from her hometown, Mobile, Alabama, to Manhattan to pursue a career in journalism. Her first jobs were at *Seventeen* magazine and then *Ladies' Home Journal*, where she edited the iconic column "Can This Marriage Be Saved?" She was the executive editor of *Redbook* and editor in chief of *Working Mother* for a decade. A founder of Take Our Daughters to Work Day, she also was the work/family contributing editor of NBC's *Today* show for five years (in the Katie Couric and Matt Lauer days). Today, she lives with husband, Walter Kirkland, in Fairhope, Alabama, and for seventeen years was an editor and consultant for *Mobile Bay* magazine.

A former regent of the Ecor Rouge Chapter, Daughters of the American Revolution, Culbreth has been recognized as a DAR national Dazzling Daughter. She utilized her genealogical sleuthing skills extensively for the book.

Her daughter and family live at Airlie Farm, Bedford, New York. Her son lives in South Orange, New Jersey.

Visit us at
www.historypress.com
....